Vegetarian Diabetic Cookbook

Nutritious and Delicious Recipes for Managing Diabetes with a Plant-Based Diet

Emily Jackson

Copyright © 2023 - All rights reserved.

The content contained within this book may not be reproduced, duplicated, or transmitted without direct written permission from the author or the publisher.

Under no circumstances will any blame or legal responsibility be held against the publisher, or author, for any damages, reparation, or monetary loss due to the information contained within this book. Either directly or indirectly.

Legal Notice:

This book is copyright protected. This book is only for personal use. You cannot amend, distribute, sell, use, quote, or paraphrase any part, or the content within this book, without the consent of the author or publisher.

Disclaimer Notice:

Please note the information contained within this document is for educational and entertainment purposes only. All effort has been executed to present accurate, up-to-date, and reliable, complete information. No warranties of any kind are declared or implied. Readers acknowledge that the author is not engaging in the rendering of legal, financial, medical, or professional advice. The content within this book has been derived from various sources. Please consult a licensed professional before attempting any techniques outlined in this book.

By reading this document, the reader agrees that under no circumstances is the author responsible for any losses, direct or indirect, which are incurred as a result of the use of the information contained within this document, including, but not limited to, — errors, omissions, or inaccuracies.

Table of Contents

WHO IS A VEGETARIAN 1
    Vegetarianism and Diabetes 3
    The Advantages of a Vegetarian Diet for People with Diabetes 4
    Nutrition Guidelines 5
    How to Balance Carbohydrates, Protein, and Fat Intake 6
    Meal Planning and Prep 7
A WEEK VEGETARIAN DIABETES MEAL PLAN RECIPES 9
    Monday 9
    Tuesday 14
    Wednesday 19
    Thursday 24
    Friday 29
    Saturday 34
    Sunday 39
    Vegetarian Diabetes Ingredient Substitutions 44
VEGETARIAN DIABETES RECIPES 45
    Breakfast Recipes 45
        Avocado Toast 45
        Greek Yogurt with Berries: 45
        Scrambled Tofu 46
        Oatmeal with Fruit and Nuts 47
        Peanut Butter and Banana Sandwich 47
        Chia Seed Pudding 48
        Tofu and Veggie Breakfast Wrap 49
        Blueberry Oat Bran Muffins 50
        Banana Walnut Pancakes 51

- Vegetable Frittata 52
- Quinoa Breakfast Bowl 53

Lunch Recipes 54
- Chickpea Salad 54
- Vegetable Stir Fry 55
- Lentil Soup 56
- Black Bean Salad 57
- Grilled Vegetable Wrap 58
- Quinoa Salad 59
- Tofu Stir Fry 60
- Chickpea Curry 61
- Avocado and Tomato Sandwich 62

Dinner Recipes 63
- Lentil and Vegetable Curry 63
- Grilled Tofu and Vegetable Kebabs 64
- Cauliflower Fried Rice 65
- Spicy Sweet Potato and Black Bean Enchiladas 66
- Quinoa and Vegetable Stir-Fry 67
- Spinach and Feta Stuffed Portobello Mushrooms 68
- Chickpea and Vegetable Tagine 69
- Zucchini Noodles with Tomato and Basil 70
- Roasted Vegetable and Quinoa Salad 71

Snacks Recipes 72
- Roasted Chickpeas 72
- Veggie and Hummus Wraps 73
- Baked Sweet Potato Fries 74
- Caprese Salad Skewers 75
- Spicy Edamame 76

Salads and Bowls for Vegetarian 77
- Kale and Brussels Sprouts Salad with Lemon Vinaigrette 77

    Quinoa and Black Bean Salad 78

    Roasted Beet and Goat Cheese Salad 80

    Buddha Bowls with Tahini Dressing.. 81

    Mediterranean Grain Bowl 83

Vegetarian Soups and Stews 85

    Vegetable and Lentil Soup 85

    Creamy Tomato Soup... 87

    Butternut Squash Soup 88

    Vegetarian Chili.. 90

    Spicy Soba Noodle Soup 92

    Roasted Chickpeas.. 93

    Guacamole with Veggie Sticks 94

    Hummus and Pita Chips 95

    Greek Yogurt and Fruit Parfait 95

    Caprese Skewers.. 96

    Veggie Roll-Ups... 96

    Roasted Almonds... 97

    No-Sugar chocolate chip cookies 97

Desert Recipes... 99

    Vegan Banana Pudding 99

    Apple Cinnamon Baked Oatmeal... 100

    Vegan Chocolate Avocado Mousse... 101

    Sugar-free Blueberry Sorbet.. 101

    Vegetarian Peanut Butter... 102

    Sugar-free Chia Seed Pudding... 102

    Vegan Pumpkin Pie 103

    Sugar-free Coconut Macaroons 104

    Sugar-free Apple Crumble 105

High-Protein Vegetarian Recipes.. 106

    Spicy Black Bean and Quinoa Bowl 106

- Lentil and Mushroom Bolognese ... 108
- Chickpea and Spinach Curry ... 110
- Tofu and Vegetable Stir Fry ... 112
- Grilled Portobello Mushroom Burgers ... 114

Low-Carb Vegetarian Recipes ... 115
- Zucchini Noodles with Avocado Pesto ... 115
- Broccoli and Cheddar Soup ... 116
- Roasted Brussels Sprouts with Tahini Sauce ... 117
- Cheesy Baked Cauliflower ... 118

Quick and Easy Vegetarian Recipes for Busy Weeknights ... 120
- One-Pot Vegetarian Chili ... 120
- 15-Minute Vegetarian Pad Thai ... 122
- Sheet Pan Vegetable Fajitas ... 124
- Chickpea Salad Sandwiches ... 126
- Creamy Avocado and White Bean Wrap ... 128

Budget-Friendly Vegetarian Recipes ... 130
- Lentil and Sweet Potato Shepherd's Pie ... 130
- Roasted Vegetable and Chickpea Salad ... 132
- Stuffed Bell Peppers ... 134
- Three-Bean Chili ... 136
- Spinach and Ricotta Stuffed Shells ... 138

Meal Prep Vegetarian Recipes for Weight Loss ... 140
- Mason Jar Salads ... 140
- Quinoa and Black Bean Bowls ... 141
- Tofu and Broccoli Stir Fry ... 142
- Stuffed Sweet Potatoes ... 144
- Greek Yogurt Parfaits ... 145

WHO IS A VEGETARIAN

A Vegetarian Diet: Types and Benefits

A vegetarian is someone who follows a diet that excludes meat, poultry, and fish, and sometimes other animal products such as eggs and dairy. There are several types of vegetarians, each with its own dietary restrictions:

- Lacto-ovo-vegetarian: This type of vegetarian includes dairy and eggs in their diet but avoids meat, poultry, and fish.
- Lacto-vegetarian: This type of vegetarian includes dairy but avoids eggs, meat, poultry, and fish.
- Ovo-vegetarian: This type of vegetarian includes eggs but avoids dairy, meat, poultry, and fish.
- Vegan: A vegan avoids all animal products, including meat, poultry, fish, dairy, eggs, honey, and any other animal-derived ingredient or product.

People choose to become vegetarian for various reasons, including ethical concerns about animal welfare, health reasons, environmental concerns, or cultural or religious beliefs.

A well-planned vegetarian diet can provide all the necessary nutrients, including protein, iron, calcium, and vitamin B12, but it is essential to ensure that the diet is diverse and includes a variety of plant-based foods. Some vegetarians may need to supplement with certain nutrients, such as vitamin B12, which is primarily found in animal products.

In general, a vegetarian diet can be a healthy and sustainable choice, but it is important to consult a healthcare provider or registered dietitian to ensure that your dietary needs are being met.

Vegetarian Diets for Diabetes

A vegetarian diet can be a healthy and effective dietary choice for people with diabetes. Studies have shown that a plant-based diet can improve blood sugar control, reduce the risk of diabetes-related complications, and promote overall health.

Here are some general guidelines for a vegetarian diabetes diet:

Focus on whole, unprocessed plant-based foods: These include fruits, vegetables, legumes, whole grains, seeds, and nuts. These foods are low in saturated fat and high in fiber, which can help regulate blood sugar levels.

Choose complex carbohydrates: Complex carbohydrates, such as whole grains, beans, and lentils, are digested more slowly than simple carbohydrates, such as white bread and sugary drinks. This slower digestion can help prevent spikes in blood sugar levels.

Monitor portion sizes: Although plant-based foods are generally healthy, it is still important to monitor portion sizes and total calorie intake, as consuming too many calories can lead to weight gain and worsen blood sugar control.

Include sources of protein: Vegetarian sources of protein include beans, lentils, tofu, tempeh, nuts, and seeds. These foods can help regulate blood sugar levels and promote feelings of fullness.

Consider supplements: People with diabetes who follow a vegetarian or vegan diet may require supplementing with vitamin B12, as it is primarily found in animal products.

It is vital to consult a healthcare provider or registered dietitian to develop a personalized meal plan that meets your individual needs and preferences.

Vegetarianism and Diabetes

Vegetarianism is a dietary prototype that excludes meat, poultry, fish, and sometimes other animal-derived ingredients such as dairy and eggs. Vegetarian diets are connected with numerous health profits, including a lower risk of high blood pressure, heart disease, obesity, and type 2 diabetes.

Diabetes is a chronic state characterized by high blood glucose levels due to the body's inability to produce or use insulin effectively. Insulin is a hormone that regulates blood sugar levels, and the pancreas produces it. A vegetarian diet can help manage type 2 diabetes by improving insulin sensitivity, reducing inflammation, and promoting weight loss.

Several studies have shown that a vegetarian diet can improve glycemic control, reduce HbA1c levels (a marker of long-term blood glucose control), and reduce the need for diabetes medications. Vegetarian diets are typically rich in fiber, whole grains, fruits, vegetables, legumes, and nuts, which can help regulate blood glucose levels.

Furthermore, vegetarian diets are generally lower in cholesterol and saturated fat, which can assist in preventing cardiovascular complications that often accompany type 2 diabetes. Plant based diets have also been shown to improve other markers of cardiovascular health, such as blood pressure and cholesterol levels.

In general, a vegetarian diet can be an effective tool for managing type 2 diabetes and reducing the risk of related health complications. However, it is essential to work with a healthcare provider or registered dietitian to ensure that nutrient needs are met and blood glucose levels are appropriately controlled.

The Advantages of a Vegetarian Diet for People with Diabetes

A vegetarian diet can offer several benefits for individuals with diabetes, which include the following:

- Improved glycemic control: A vegetarian diet is typically high in fiber, whole grains, fruits, vegetables, legumes, and nuts, which can help regulate blood glucose levels. These foods are also low on the glycemic index, meaning they do not cause a significant increase in blood glucose levels.

- Weight management: A vegetarian diet is often lower in calories and saturated fat than a diet that includes meat, making it an effective tool for weight loss or management. This is especially significant for individuals with type 2 diabetes who may be overweight or obese.

- Reduced risk of cardiovascular disease: Individuals with diabetes are at an increased risk of developing cardiovascular disease. A vegetarian diet is typically lower in saturated fat and cholesterol, which can help decrease the risk of heart disease.

- Improved insulin sensitivity: A vegetarian diet is rich in plant-based protein and fiber, which can help improve insulin sensitivity, making it easier for the body to use insulin effectively.

- Reduced need for diabetes medications: Some studies have shown that a vegetarian diet can improve glycemic control to the extent that diabetes medications may not be needed or can be reduced.
- Improved overall health: A vegetarian diet is rich in nutrients, vitamins, and minerals that can help improve overall health, reduce inflammation, and prevent chronic diseases.

It is important to note that not all vegetarian diets are equal. A diet that is high in processed foods, refined carbohydrates, and sugar can still lead to poor blood glucose control and other health problems. Therefore, it is essential to work with a healthcare provider or registered dietitian to develop a balanced, nutrient-rich vegetarian diet that meets individual needs and preferences.

Nutrition Guidelines

When following a vegetarian diet, it's important to ensure that you're getting all the nutrients your body needs. Here are some general nutrition guidelines to follow:

Protein: Vegetarian sources of protein include legumes (beans, lentils, chickpeas), nuts, seeds, and soy products (tofu, tempeh, soy milk). Aim for 2-3 servings of protein-rich foods per day.

Calcium: Vegetarian sources of calcium include fortified plant milks, tofu prepare with calcium sulfate, leafy green vegetables, and some nuts and seeds. Aim for 2-3 servings of rich calcium foods per day.

Iron: Vegetarian sources of iron include leafy green vegetables, fortified grains and cereals, beans, lentils, and some nuts and seeds. Pairing iron-rich foods with a source of vitamin C (such as citrus fruits or bell peppers) can help improve absorption. Aim for 2-3 servings of iron-rich foods per day.

Vitamin B12: Vitamin B12 is only naturally found in animal products, so vegetarians may need to supplement or consume fortified foods (such as plant milks, breakfast cereals, and nutritional yeast) to ensure adequate intake.

Omega-3 fatty acids: Vegetarian sources of omega-3 fatty acids include flaxseeds, chia seeds, hemp seeds, walnuts, and algae-based supplements.

Fiber: Vegetarian diets are generally high in fiber, which can help regulate blood glucose levels and promote satiety. Aim for 25-35g of fiber daily.

Balanced meals: Aim to include different foods at each meal, including whole grains, protein rich foods, and plenty of fruits and vegetables.

It's also important to monitor blood glucose levels regularly and work with a healthcare provider or registered dietitian to adjust your diet as needed.

How to Balance Carbohydrates, Protein, and Fat Intake

Balancing carbohydrate, protein, and fat intake is important for overall health and can be particularly important for people with diabetes who need to manage their blood glucose levels. Here are some tips for balancing these macronutrients:

Carbohydrates: Carbohydrates are an essential source of energy for the body and should make up 45-65% of total calorie intake. However, not all carbohydrates are created equal. Aim for complex carbohydrates (such as whole grains, vegetables, and fruits) that are rich in fiber and do not cause a significant spike in blood glucose levels. Limit simple carbohydrates (such as sugary drinks, candy, and baked goods) that can cause a rapid increase in blood glucose levels.

Protein: Protein is important for building and repairing tissues and should make up 10-35% of total calorie intake. Aim for a variety of protein sources, including legumes, nuts, seeds, and soy products.

Fat: Fat is important for absorbing certain vitamins, providing insulation, and protecting organs. Fat should make up 20-35% of total calorie intake. Aim for healthy sources of fat, such as nuts, seeds, avocado, and fatty fish (if you include fish in your diet). Limit saturated and trans fats (found in animal products, fried foods, and some processed foods).

When planning meals, aim to include a balance of protein, carbohydrates, and fat. For example, a meal might include a serving of whole grains (carbohydrates), a serving of legumes (protein), and a serving of roasted vegetables with olive oil (fat). Snacks can also be balanced by pairing carbohydrates with a source of protein or fat. For example, a piece of fruit with a handful of nuts or a serving of whole-grain crackers with hummus.

It's important to work with a healthcare provider or registered dietitian to determine the appropriate balance of macronutrients for your individual needs and health goals.

Meal Planning and Prep

Meal planning and prep can be helpful strategies for maintaining a healthy vegetarian diet, managing blood glucose levels, and saving time during the week.

Set aside some time each week to plan meals and snacks for the week ahead. Consider your schedule, food preferences, and any dietary restrictions or health goals.

Once you've planned your meals, make a shopping list and stick to it. This can help prevent impulse purchases and ensure that you have all the ingredients you need on hand.

Consider batch cooking large batches of grains, legumes, or roasted vegetables at the beginning of the week. These can be used as the base for meals all through the week and can save time on cooking and cleanup.

Wash and chop vegetables ahead of time to save time during meal prep. Store them in airtight containers in the fridge for easy access.

Slow cookers can be a convenient way to prepare meals ahead of time. Simply add ingredients in the morning, and dinner will be ready when you get home.

If you're on-the-go during the day, pack meals and snacks in advance to prevent unhealthy impulse purchases. Consider using a bento box or other reusable containers for easy transportation.

Eating a vegetarian diet doesn't have to be boring. Experiment with new recipes and ingredients to keep meals interesting and flavorful.

Remember, it's important to work with a healthcare provider or registered dietitian to develop a personalized meal plan that meets your individual needs and health goals.

A WEEK VEGETARIAN DIABETES MEAL PLAN RECIPES

Monday

BREAKFAST:

Oatmeal with Sliced Banana and Chopped Walnuts

Ingredients:

- 1/2 cup rolled oats
- 1 cup water or unsweetened almond milk
- Pinch of salt
- 1/2 medium banana, sliced
- 1 tablespoon chopped walnuts

Instructions:

1. Combine the water or almond milk, oats, and salt in a saucepan.
2. Bring to a boil, then reduce heat and simmer for 5-10 minutes, stirring occasionally.
3. Once the oatmeal is cooked to your desired consistency, remove from heat.
4. Serve the oatmeal in a bowl and top with the sliced banana and chopped walnuts.
5. Enjoy your healthy and delicious breakfast!

SNACKS:

Carrot Sticks with Hummus

Ingredients:
- 2-3 medium carrots, peeled and sliced into sticks
- 1/4 cup hummus

Instructions:
1. Wash and peel the carrots, then slice them into sticks.
2. Scoop hummus about ¼ cup into a small bowl.
3. Arrange the carrot sticks around the bowl of hummus.
4. Dip the carrot sticks into the hummus and enjoy as a healthy and delicious snack!

LUNCH:

Lentil Soup with Whole-Grain Bread

Ingredients:
- 1 tablespoon olive oil
- 1 medium onion, diced
- 2 cloves garlic, minced
- 2 carrots, diced
- 2 celery stalks, diced
- 1 teaspoon ground cumin
- 1/2 teaspoon ground coriander
- 1/4 teaspoon red pepper flakes
- 1 cup dry brown lentils, rinsed and drained
- 4 cups vegetable broth
- 1 (14.5-ounce) can diced tomatoes

- Salt and pepper, to taste
- Fresh parsley, chopped (optional)
- 2 slices of whole-grain bread

Instructions:
1. In a large pot, heat the olive oil over medium heat.
2. Add the onion and garlic and sauté until the onion is translucent, about 5 minutes.
3. Add the carrots and celery and continue to sauté for another 5 minutes.
4. Add the cumin, coriander, and red pepper flakes and stir to combine.
5. Add the lentils, vegetable broth, and diced tomatoes to the pot.
6. Bring the soup to a boil, then lower the heat and simmer for 30-40 minutes, or until the lentils are tender.
7. Season with pepper and salt to taste and garnish with fresh parsley, if desired.
8. Serve the lentil soup with whole-grain bread on the side for a delicious and filling meal. Enjoy!

DINNER:
Tofu Stir-Fry with Mixed Vegetables and Brown Rice

Ingredients:
- 1 cup uncooked brown rice
- 1 tablespoon vegetable oil
- 1 (14-ounce) block of extra-firm tofu, drained and pressed
- 1 red bell pepper, sliced
- 1 green bell pepper, sliced
- 1 small head of broccoli, chopped into florets
- 1 medium carrot, peeled and sliced
- 1/2 cup sliced mushrooms
- 2 garlic cloves, minced
- 1/4 cup low-sodium soy sauce
- 2 tablespoons hoisin sauce
- 1 tablespoon cornstarch
- Salt and pepper, to taste

Instructions:
1. Cook the brown rice according to package instructions.
2. Heat the vegetable oil over medium-high heat in a large skillet.
3. Add the sliced tofu and cook until lightly browned, about 5-7 minutes.
4. Remove the tofu from the skillet and set aside.
5. Add the bell peppers, broccoli, carrot, mushrooms, and garlic to the skillet and stir-fry for 5-7 minutes, or until the vegetables are tender-crisp.
6. Whisk together the soy sauce in a small bowl, hoisin sauce, and cornstarch.

7. Add the tofu that has already been cooked back into the skillet and pour the soy sauce mixture over everything.
8. Stir to coat the tofu and vegetables in the sauce, and cook for an additional 1-2 minutes, or until the sauce has thickened.
9. Season with salt and pepper to taste.
10. Serve the tofu stir-fry over brown rice for a nutritious and tasty meal. Enjoy!

Tuesday

BREAKFAST:

Greek Yogurt with Mixed Berries and Sliced Almonds

Ingredients:

- 1 cup plain Greek yogurt
- 1/2 cup mixed berries (such as strawberries, blueberries, raspberries, and blackberries)
- 1 tablespoon sliced almonds

Instructions:

1. Wash the berries and slice any larger berries into smaller pieces.
2. Spoon the Greek yogurt into a bowl.
3. Top the yogurt with the mixed berries and sliced almonds.
4. Enjoy your healthy and protein-packed breakfast!

SNACKS:

Sliced Apple with Peanut Butter

Ingredients:

- 1 medium apple, sliced
- 2 tablespoons peanut butter

Instructions:

1. Wash and slice the apple into thin rounds.
2. Scoop peanut butter about 2 tablespoons into a small bowl.
3. Dip the apple slices into the peanut butter and enjoy as a healthy and satisfying snack.

LUNCH:

Chickpea and Vegetable Curry with Quinoa

Ingredients:

- 1 tablespoon olive oil
- 1 medium onion, diced
- 2 cloves garlic, minced
- 1 red bell pepper, diced
- 1 small head of cauliflower, chopped into florets
- 1 medium zucchini, chopped
- 1 (15-ounce) can chickpeas
- 1 (14.5-ounce) can diced tomatoes
- 1 tablespoon curry powder
- 1 teaspoon ground cumin
- 1/4 teaspoon red pepper flakes
- Salt and pepper, to taste
- 1 cup quinoa
- 2 cups water or vegetable broth
- Fresh cilantro, chopped (optional)

Instructions:

1. In a large pot, heat the olive oil over medium heat.
2. Add the onion and garlic and sauté until the onion is translucent, about 5 minutes.
3. Add the red bell pepper, cauliflower, and zucchini and continue to sauté for another 5 minutes.
4. Add the chickpeas, diced tomatoes, curry powder, cumin, and red pepper flakes to the pot.
5. Stir everything together and bring the mixture to a boil.

6. Reduce heat and let the curry simmer for 20-30 minutes, or until the vegetables are tender.
7. While the curry is cooking, rinse the quinoa in a strainer and add it to a medium pot with 2 cups of water or vegetable broth.
8. Bring the quinoa to a boil, then lower heat and let it simmer for 15-20 minutes, or until all the water is absorbed.
9. Fluff the quinoa with a fork and season with salt and pepper to taste.
10. Serve the chickpea and vegetable curry over a bed of quinoa and garnish with fresh cilantro, if desired. Enjoy!

DINNER:
Stuffed Bell Peppers with Tomato Sauce and Brown Rice

Ingredients:
- 4 bell peppers, any color
- 1 cup uncooked brown rice
- 2 cups water or vegetable broth
- 1 tablespoon olive oil
- 1 medium onion, diced
- 2 cloves garlic, minced
- 1 small zucchini, diced
- 1 small yellow squash, diced
- 1 (14.5-ounce) can diced tomatoes
- 1 teaspoon dried oregano
- 1 teaspoon dried basil
- Salt and pepper, to taste

Instructions:
1. Preheat the oven to 375°F (190°C).
2. Cut the tops off of the bell peppers and remove the seeds and membranes from inside.
3. Rinse the brown rice in a strainer and add it to a medium pot with 2 cups of water or vegetable broth.
4. Bring the rice to a boil, then reduce heat to low and let it simmer for 35-40 minutes, or until all the water is absorbed and the rice is tender.
5. While the rice is cooking, heat the olive oil in a large skillet over medium heat.
6. Add the diced onion and garlic to the skillet and sauté for 2-3 minutes, or until the onion is translucent.

7. Add the diced zucchini and yellow squash to the skillet and continue to sauté for another 5-7 minutes, or until the vegetables are tender.
8. Add the oregano, diced tomatoes, basil, pepper and salt to the skillet and stir everything together.
9. Add the brown rice that's already cooked to the skillet and stir to combine all the ingredients.
10. Stuff each of the bell peppers with the rice and vegetable mixture.
11. Place the stuffed peppers in a baking dish and pour a little bit of tomato sauce over each pepper.
12. Cover the baking dish with foil and bake for 35-40 minutes, or until the peppers are tender.
13. Serve the stuffed bell peppers with extra tomato sauce on top, if desired. Enjoy!

Wednesday

BREAKFAST:

Smoothie with Spinach, Banana, Almond Milk, and Protein Powder

Ingredients:
- 1 cup unsweetened almond milk
- 1 ripe banana, peeled
- 1 cup fresh spinach leaves
- 1 scoop vanilla protein powder
- 1 cup ice cubes

Instructions:
1. Add the almond milk to a blender.
2. Add the banana, spinach, protein powder, and ice cubes to the blender.
3. Blend all of the ingredients together on high speed until the smoothie is completely smooth and creamy.
4. Taste the smoothie and add additional sweetener or ice cubes as needed to reach your desired taste and texture.
5. Pour the smoothie into a glass and enjoy right away.

SNACKS:

Air-Popped Popcorn

Ingredients:
- 1/2 cup popcorn kernels
- 1-2 tablespoons vegetable oil or butter (optional)
- Salt, to taste

Instructions:
1. Add the popcorn kernels to an air popper.
2. If you want to add oil or butter for flavor, you can melt the butter or heat the oil in a small saucepan until melted and then drizzle it over the popcorn.
3. Turn on the air popper and let the kernels pop until there is a 2-3 second delay between pops.
4. Turn off the air popper and remove the popcorn from the popper.
5. Season the popcorn with salt to taste, and serve. Enjoy!

LUNCH:
Black Bean and Sweet Potato Chili with Whole-Grain Bread

Ingredients:
- 1 tablespoon olive oil
- 1 medium onion, diced
- 2 cloves garlic, minced
- 2 medium sweet potatoes, peeled and cubed
- 1 (15-ounce) can black beans, drained and rinsed
- 1 (14.5-ounce) can diced tomatoes
- 1 tablespoon chili powder
- 1 teaspoon ground cumin
- 1/2 teaspoon smoked paprika
- 1/2 teaspoon salt
- 2 cups water or vegetable broth
- Whole-grain bread, for serving

Instructions:
1. Heat the olive oil in a large pot over medium heat.
2. Add the diced onion and minced garlic to the pot and sauté for 2-3 minutes, or until the onion is translucent.
3. Add the cubed sweet potatoes to the pot and stir everything together.
4. Add the black beans, diced tomatoes, chili powder, smoked paprika, ground cumin, and salt to the pot.
5. Pour the water or vegetable broth over the ingredients in the pot and stir everything together.
6. Bring the chili to a simmer and let it cook for 20-25 minutes, or until the sweet potatoes are tender and the flavors have melded together.
7. Serve the chili hot with slices of whole-grain bread on the side. Enjoy!

DINNER:
Zucchini Noodles with Tomato Sauce and Grilled Tofu

Ingredients:
- 2 medium zucchinis
- 1 (14.5-ounce) can diced tomatoes
- 1/2 onion, diced
- 2 cloves garlic, minced
- 1 tablespoon olive oil
- 1/2 teaspoon dried basil
- 1/2 teaspoon dried oregano
- Salt and pepper, to taste
- 8 ounces firm tofu, drained and pressed
- Cooking spray

Instructions:
1. Use a spiralizer to make zucchini noodles out of the zucchinis. Set the noodles aside.
2. In a medium saucepan, sauté the diced onion and minced garlic in olive oil over medium heat until the onion is translucent.
3. Add the diced tomatoes, dried basil, dried oregano, salt, and pepper to the saucepan with the onion and garlic. Stir all together and allow the sauce simmer for 10-15 minutes.
4. While the tomato sauce is simmering, preheat a grill pan or outdoor grill to mediumhigh heat.
5. Slice the drained and pressed tofu into 1/2-inch thick pieces.
6. Spray the tofu pieces with cooking spray and grill them for 3-4 minutes per side, or until they have grill marks and are heated through.

7. To serve, place the zucchini noodles on a plate or in a bowl. Top the noodles with a generous scoop of tomato sauce and a few pieces of grilled tofu. Enjoy!

Thursday

BREAKFAST:

Scrambled Eggs with Avocado and Whole-Grain Toast

Ingredients:

- 2 large eggs
- 1/4 avocado, diced
- Salt and pepper, to taste
- 1 slice whole-grain bread
- Butter or cooking spray, for cooking

Instructions:

1. Crack the eggs into a small bowl and whisk them together with a fork. Add salt and pepper to taste.
2. Heat a non-stick skillet over medium heat. Add butter or cooking spray to the skillet.
3. Pour the whisked eggs into the skillet and use a spatula to gently scramble them as they cook.
4. Once the eggs are almost fully cooked, add the diced avocado to the skillet and continue to scramble everything together until the eggs are fully cooked and the avocado is heated through.
5. Toast the slice of whole-grain bread.
6. Serve the scrambled eggs and avocado on top of the toasted bread. Enjoy!

SNACKS:
Sliced Apple with Peanut Butter

Ingredients:
- 1 large apple
- 2-3 tablespoons of peanut butter
- Optional toppings: raisins, cinnamon, honey, or granola

Instructions:
1. Wash the apple and slice it into thin slices using a sharp knife or apple slicer.
2. Place the slices on a plate or serving dish.
3. Scoop the peanut butter into a small bowl or ramekin.
4. Dip each apple slice into the peanut butter, or spread a generous amount of peanut butter onto each slice.
5. If desired, sprinkle toppings such as raisins, cinnamon, honey, or granola over the peanut butter.
6. Serve and enjoy as a healthy and delicious snack!

LUNCH:

Lentil and Vegetable Salad with Whole-Grain Pita

Ingredients:

- 1 cup cooked lentils (can use canned or cook from dry)
- 2 cups mixed vegetables (such as cucumber, bell pepper, cherry tomatoes, and redonion), chopped
- 1/4 cup crumbled feta cheese
- 2 tablespoons chopped fresh herbs (such as parsley, basil, or mint)
- 2 tablespoons extra-virgin olive oil
- 1 tablespoon fresh lemon juice
- Salt and pepper to taste
- 2 whole-grain pitas

Instructions:

1. If using dry lentils, rinse them in a fine mesh strainer and place in a pot with 2 cups of water. Bring to a boil, reduce heat to a simmer, and cook until tender, about 20-25 minutes. Drain any surplus water and set aside.
2. Chop your vegetables of choice into bite-sized pieces and add to a large mixing bowl along with the cooked lentils.
3. In a small mixing bowl, whisk together the olive oil, lemon juice, salt, and pepper. Pour over the lentil and vegetable mixture and toss to coat.
4. Sprinkle the crumbled feta cheese and fresh herbs over the top of the salad and gently toss again.
5. To serve, cut the whole-grain pitas in half and warm them up in the oven or microwave. Fill each pita half with the lentil and vegetable salad.
6. Enjoy your healthy and delicious Lentil and Vegetable Salad with Whole-Grain Pita!

DINNER:

Spaghetti Squash with Tomato Sauce and Vegetarian Meatballs

Ingredients:

- 1 spaghetti squash
- 1 can of crushed tomatoes (28 oz)
- 1 onion, chopped
- 2 cloves of garlic, minced
- 2 tbsp olive oil
- Salt and pepper to taste
- Vegetarian meatballs (store-bought or homemade)

Instructions:

1. Preheat your oven to 375°F (190°C).
2. Cut the spaghetti squash equally and scrape out the pulp and seeds.
3. Brush the inside of each half with olive oil and shower with salt and pepper.
4. On a baking sheet, place the two cut face down and bake for 35-40 minutes or until the flesh is tender.
5. While the spaghetti squash is cooking, prepare the tomato sauce.
6. In a saucepan, Heat 2 tablespoons of olive oil over medium heat.
7. Add the chopped onion and cook for 3-4 minutes until softened.
8. Add the minced garlic and cook for an extra minute until fragrant.
9. Pour in the can of crushed tomatoes and stir to combine.

10. Bring the sauce to a simmer and let it cook for 10-15 minutes or until it has thickened slightly.
11. Season the tomato sauce with salt and pepper to taste.
12. Prepare the vegetarian meatballs according to package instructions or use your favorite homemade recipe.
13. Once the spaghetti squash is cooked, remove it from the oven and let it cool slightly.
14. Use a fork to scratch the flesh of the squash into long strands.
15. Place the spaghetti squash strands in a bowl and top with the tomato sauce and vegetarian meatballs.
16. Serve and enjoy!

Friday

BREAKFAST:

Cottage Cheese with Mixed Berries and Chopped Nuts

Ingredients:
- 1 cup cottage cheese
- 1/2 cup mixed berries (blueberries, strawberries, raspberries, blackberries)
- 1/4 cup chopped nuts (walnuts, almonds, pecans)
- 1 tbsp honey (optional)

Instructions:
1. Wash the mixed berries and remove any stems. Cut the strawberries into bite-sized pieces if they are large.
2. In a bowl, mix the cottage cheese and honey (if using) together.
3. Add the mixed berries to the cottage cheese mixture and gently mix.
4. Top the mixture with chopped nuts.
5. Serve immediately or refrigerate until ready to eat. Enjoy!

SNACKS:

Celery Sticks with Almond Butter

Ingredients:

- 4 celery stalks
- 4 tbsp almond butter
- 1 tbsp honey (optional)
- 1 tbsp chia seeds (optional)

Instructions:

1. Wash the celery stalks and trim off the ends. Cut the stalks into 3-4 inch pieces.
2. In a small bowl, mix the honey and almond butter (if using) together until well combined.
3. Spread the almond butter mixture into the hollow part of each celery stick.
4. Sprinkle chia seeds on top of the almond butter (if using).
5. Serve right away or refrigerate until set to eat. Enjoy as a healthy snack or appetizer!

LUNCH:

Quinoa and Black Bean Salad with Mixed Greens

Ingredients:

- 1 cup quinoa
- 1 can black beans, rinsed and drained
- 1 red bell pepper, chopped
- 1/2 red onion, chopped
- 1/4 cup fresh cilantro, chopped
- 2 bsp olive oil
- 2 tbsp lime juice
- Salt and pepper to taste
- Mixed greens for serving

Instructions:

1. Rinse the quinoa in cold water and drain. In a medium saucepan, boil 2 cups of water. Add the quinoa and reduce heat. Cover and simmer for 15-20 minutes, until the quinoa is tender and the water has been absorbed. Fluff with a fork and set aside to cool.
2. In a large bowl, mix together the cooked quinoa, black beans, red bell pepper, red onion, and cilantro.
3. In a small bowl, whisk together the olive oil, lime juice, salt, and pepper. The dressing should be pour over the quinoa mixture and throw until well coated.
4. Serve the quinoa salad over a bed of mixed greens. Enjoy as a healthy and delicious meal!

DINNER:

Vegetable Stir-Fry with Brown Rice and Tofu

Ingredients:

For the stir-fry:
- 1 block of firm tofu, drained and cut into small cubes
- 1 tbsp vegetable oil
- 1 red bell pepper, sliced
- 1 yellow onion, sliced
- 2 cups sliced vegetables of your choice (such as mushrooms, broccoli, carrots, or snappeas)
- 2 cloves garlic, minced
- 1 inch piece of ginger, grated
- Salt and pepper, to taste

For the brown rice:
- 1 cup brown rice2 cups water

For the sauce:
- 1/4 cup soy sauce
- 2 tbsp honey
- 1 tbsp cornstarch
- 1/2 tsp sesame oil
- 1/2 tsp red pepper flakes

Instructions:
1. Rinse the brown rice and add it to a medium-sized pot with 2 cups of water. Bring the rice to a boil, then reduce the heat to low and cover the pot. Cook for 40-45 minutes, or until the rice is tender and the water absorbed.

2. While the rice is cooking, prepare the stir-fry. In a large skillet or wok, heat the vegetable oil over medium-high heat. Add the tofu cubes and cook for 5-7 minutes, or until golden brown. Remove the tofu from the skillet and set aside.
3. Add the sliced red bell pepper, yellow onion, and any other vegetables of your choice to the skillet. Cook for 5-7 minutes, or until the veggies are tender.
4. Add the minced garlic and grated ginger to the skillet and cook for 1-2 minutes, or until fragrant.
5. In a small bowl, mix the honey, soy sauce, cornstarch, sesame oil, and red pepper flakes together to make the sauce.
6. Add the cooked tofu back to the skillet with the vegetables. Pour the sauce over the tofu and vegetables, and stir to coat everything evenly. Cook for an additional 2-3 minutes, or until the sauce has thickened.
7. Serve the vegetable stir-fry over the cooked brown rice.

Saturday

BREAKFAST:
Whole-Grain Waffles with Mixed Berries and Maple Syrup

Ingredients:

- 1 cup whole wheat flour
- 1/2 cup all-purpose flour
- 2 tbsp sugar
- 2 tsp baking powder
- 1/2 tsp salt
- 1 1/2 cups milk
- 2 eggs
- 2 tbsp vegetable oil
- 1 tsp vanilla extract
- 1 cup mixed berries (such as blueberries, strawberries, and raspberries)
- Maple syrup, for serving

Instructions:

1. In an outsized mixing bowl, whisk together the whole wheat flour, all-purpose flour, sugar, baking powder, and salt.
2. In a different bowl, beat the eggs and then whisk in the milk, vegetable oil, and vanilla extract.
3. Pour the wet ingredients into the dry ingredients and stir until just combined. Be careful not to over mix.
4. Heat a waffle iron and evenly grease it with melted butter or cooking spray.

5. Pour the batter on top of the waffle iron according to the manufacturer's instructions, and cook until the waffles are golden brown and crispy.
6. While the waffles are cooking, rinse and slice the mixed berries.
7. Serve the waffles hot with the mixed berries and maple syrup.
8. Enjoy your delicious and nutritious whole-grain waffles with mixed berries and maple syrup!

SNACKS:

Roasted Almonds

Ingredients:
- 2 cups raw almonds
- 1 tsp olive oil
- 1/2 tsp salt

Instructions:
1. Preheat the oven to 350°F (175°C).
2. Line a baking sheet with parchment paper.
3. In a bowl, mix the almonds, olive oil, and salt until the almonds are coated evenly.
4. Spread the almonds in a single layer on the arranged baking sheet.
5. Roast the almonds in the preheated oven for 10-12 minutes, or until they are golden brown and fragrant.
6. Remove the almonds from the oven and let them cool completely before serving.
7. Enjoy your delicious and crunchy roasted almonds as a snack or add them to your favorite recipes!

LUNCH:
Vegetable Lasagna with Side Salad

Ingredients:

For the lasagna:

- 1 package lasagna noodles
- 2 tbsp olive oil
- 1 onion, chopped
- 2 cloves garlic, minced
- 2 cups sliced vegetables of your choice (such as mushrooms, zucchini, eggplant, or bell peppers)
- 1 jar tomato sauce
- 1 cup ricotta cheese
- 2 cups shredded mozzarella cheese
- 1/4 cup grated parmesan cheese
- Salt and pepper, to taste

For the side salad:

- 4 cups mixed greens
- 1 cucumber, sliced
- 1 tomato, chopped
- 1/4 red onion, sliced
- 1/4 cup balsamic vinaigrette dressing

Instructions:

1. Preheat the oven to 375°F (190°C).
2. Cook the lasagna noodles according to the package instructions. Drain and set aside.

3. In an outsized skillet, heat the olive oil over medium-high heat. Add the chopped onion and garlic and cook for 1-2 minutes, or until fragrant.
4. Add the sliced vegetables to the skillet and cook for 5-7 minutes, or until tender.
5. Add the tomato sauce to the skillet and stir to combine.
6. Using different bowl, mix together the ricotta cheese, 1 cup of shredded mozzarella cheese, and ¼ cup of grated parmesan cheese. Season with salt and pepper to taste.
7. In a baking dish, spread a layer of the tomato sauce and vegetable mixture on the bottom. Add a layer of lasagna noodles on top, followed by a layer of the cheese mixture. Repeat these layers until all the ingredients have been used up.
8. Top the lasagna with the remaining shredded mozzarella cheese.
9. Cover the baking dish with foil and bake in the preheated oven for 25 minutes.
10. Remove the foil and bake for an additional 10-15 minutes, or until the cheese is melted and bubbly.
11. While the lasagna is baking, prepare the side salad. In a large bowl, toss together the mixed greens, sliced cucumber, chopped tomato, and sliced red onion. Drizzle the balsamic vinaigrette dressing over the top and toss to coat.
12. Serve the vegetable lasagna hot with the side salad.
13. Enjoy your delicious and hearty vegetable lasagna with a side salad!

DINNER:

Avocado Toast with Scrambled Eggs

Ingredients:
- 2 slices of whole-grain bread
- 1 ripe avocado
- 1 tbsp lemon juice
- Salt and pepper, to taste
- 2 eggs
- 1 tbsp butter or olive oil
- Optional toppings: red pepper flakes, chopped chives, sliced tomatoes

Instructions:
1. Toast the slices of bread until golden brown.
2. While the bread is toasting, cut the avocado in half, remove the pit, and scoop the flesh into a bowl.
3. Add the lemon juice, salt, and pepper to the bowl and mash the avocado with a fork until smooth.
4. In a small bowl, mix the eggs with a pinch of salt and pepper together.
5. Heat a small skillet over medium heat and add the butter or olive oil. Once the butter is melted or the oil is hot, pour in the egg mixture.
6. Cook the eggs, stirring occasionally, until they are scrambled and fully cooked.
7. Spread the mashed avocado onto the toasted bread slices.
8. Spoon the scrambled eggs on top of the avocado toast.
9. Top with optional toppings, if desired.
10. Enjoy your delicious and nutritious avocado toast with scrambled eggs!

Sunday

BREAKFAST:
Carrot Sticks with Hummus

Ingredients:

- 4-5 large carrots, peeled and cut into sticks
- 1 cup canned chickpeas, drained and rinsed
- 1 garlic clove, minced
- 1/4 cup tahini
- 2 tbsp lemon juice
- 2 tbsp olive oil
- 1/4 tsp cumin
- Salt and pepper, to taste
- Water, as needed

Instructions:

1. Peel and cut the carrots into sticks.
2. In a small bowl, mix together the garlic, tahini, lemon juice, olive oil, cumin, and a pinch of salt and pepper.
3. Add the chickpeas to a food processor and pulse until finely chopped.
4. Add the tahini mixture to the food processor with the chickpeas and pulse until smooth.
5. If the hummus is too thick, add a little bit of water until you reach your desired consistency.
6. Transfer the hummus to a bowl and serve with the carrot sticks.
7. Enjoy your healthy and delicious snack of carrot sticks with hummus!

LUNCH:

Minestrone Soup with Whole-Grain Bread

Ingredients:
- 1 tbsp olive oil
- 1 onion, diced
- 2 cloves garlic, minced
- 2 carrots, diced
- 2 celery stalks, diced 1 can diced tomatoes
- 1 can kidney beans, drained and rinsed
- 6 cups vegetable broth
- 1 cup small pasta, such as elbow or ditalini
- 2 cups chopped fresh spinach or kale
- 1 tbsp chopped fresh basil
- Salt and pepper, to taste
- 4 slices of whole-grain bread

Instructions:
1. Heat the olive oil in a large pot over medium heat. Add the diced onion and garlic and cook until softened, about 3-4 minutes.
2. Add the diced celery and carrots to the pot and cook for another 5 minutes.
3. Pour in the can of diced tomatoes, drained kidney beans, and vegetable broth. Bring the soup to a boil, then reduce the heat and let it simmer for 15-20 minutes.
4. Add the small pasta to the soup and let it cook for an additional 10-12 minutes, or until the pasta is tender.
5. Stir in the chopped spinach or kale and fresh basil. Season the soup with salt and pepper to taste.

6. While the soup is cooking, slice the whole-grain bread into thick slices and toast them in a toaster or under the broiler in the oven.
7. Ladle the minestrone soup into bowls and serve with the toasted whole-grain bread on the side.
8. Enjoy your warm and hearty bowl of minestrone soup with whole-grain bread!

DINNER:
Mushroom and Vegetable Risotto

Ingredients:
- 6 cups vegetable broth
- 2 tbsp olive oil
- 1 onion, chopped
- 2 garlic cloves, minced1
- 1/2 cups Arborio rice
- 1/2 cup white wine (optional)
- 1 cup sliced mushrooms
- 1 cup chopped vegetables, such as zucchini, bell pepper, or asparagus
- 1/2 cup grated Parmesan cheese
- Salt and pepper, to taste
- 2 tbsp chopped fresh parsley

Instructions:
1. Heat the vegetable broth in a small saucepan over low heat.
2. Heat the olive oil in an outsized pot over medium heat. Add the chopped onion and garlic and cook until softened, about 3-4 minutes.
3. Add the Arborio rice to the pot and stir to coat it with the olive oil. Cook the rice for 2-3 minutes, or until it starts to turn translucent.
4. If using, pour in the white wine and cook until it has been absorbed by the rice.
5. Ladle a ladleful of the warm vegetable broth into the pot with the rice and stir until it has been absorbed. Continue

to add the broth one ladleful at a time, stirring constantly, until the rice is tender and creamy. This will take about 20-25 minutes.

6. As the risotto is cooking, heat a separate pan over medium heat and add the sliced mushrooms and chopped vegetables. Cook until tender and slightly browned, about 57 minutes.

7. When the risotto is nearly done, stir in the cooked mushrooms and vegetables, grated Parmesan cheese, and a pinch of salt and pepper. Taste and adjust seasoning as needed.

8. Serve the mushroom and vegetable risotto immediately, garnished with chopped fresh parsley.

9. Enjoy your delicious and satisfying bowl of mushroom and vegetable risotto!

Vegetarian Diabetes Ingredient Substitutions

For vegetarians with diabetes, it is important to make ingredient substitutions to maintain blood sugar control while still ensuring adequate nutrition. Here are some substitutions to consider:

Carbohydrates: Vegetarian diets can be high in carbohydrates, which can cause blood sugar spikes. To lower the amount of carbohydrates, consider substituting starchy vegetables like potatoes, corn, and peas with non-starchy vegetables like leafy greens, broccoli, cauliflower, and zucchini.

Protein: Protein is essential for vegetarians, but not all protein sources are created equal. Consider replacing high-carbohydrate protein sources like beans and lentils with low carbohydrate sources like tofu, tempeh, and seitan.

Fats: Healthy fats are an important part of a balanced vegetarian diet, but it's important to choose the right kinds of fats. Replace saturated fats like butter and cheese with unsaturated fats like olive oil, avocado, and nuts.

Sweeteners: Avoid high-sugar sweeteners like table sugar and honey, and instead opt for low glycemic sweeteners like stevia, erythritol, or monk fruit.

Grains: When choosing grains, look for whole grains that the fiber are high, such as quinoa, brown rice, and barley. Avoid refined grains like white rice and pasta, which can increase the blood sugar levels.

By making these ingredient substitutions, vegetarians with diabetes can enjoy a healthy and satisfying diet that supports optimal blood sugar control. It's always a good idea to talk to a registered dietitian or healthcare professional to help you create a personalized meal plan that meets your individual needs.

VEGETARIAN DIABETES RECIPES

Breakfast Recipes

Avocado Toast

Ingredients:
- 1 slice of whole grain bread
- 1/2 avocado
- Salt and pepper
- 1 teaspoon of lemon juice

Instructions:
1. Toast the slice of bread.
2. Mash the avocado in a bowl and add salt, pepper, and lemon juice.
3. Spread the avocado mixture on top of the toast.

Greek Yogurt with Berries:

Ingredients:
- 1 cup of Greek yogurt
- 1/2 cup of berries (strawberries, blueberries, raspberries)

Instructions:
1. Place the Greek yogurt in a bowl.
2. Add the berries on top.

Scrambled Tofu

Ingredients:
- 1/2 block of tofu
- 1/2 onion
- 1/2 red pepper
- 1/2 teaspoon of garlic powder
- 1/2 teaspoon of onion powder
- Salt and pepper

Instructions:
1. Mash the tofu with a fork.
2. Chop the onion and red pepper.
3. Heat a non-stick skillet over medium-high heat.
4. Add the onion and red pepper to the skillet and sauté for 3-4 minutes.
5. Add the mashed tofu to the skillet and cook for 5-6 minutes, stirring occasionally.
6. Add onion powder, garlic powder, salt, and pepper to the skillet and cook for an additional minute.

Oatmeal with Fruit and Nuts

Ingredients:
- 1/2 cup of rolled oats
- 1/2 cup of water
- 1/2 cup of almond milk
- 1/4 cup of chopped nuts (almonds, walnuts, pecans)
- 1/2 cup of chopped fruit (apple, banana, berries)

Instructions:
1. In a small pot, bring the water and almond milk to a boil.
2. Add the oats to the pot and reduce heat to low.
3. Cook for 5-7 minutes, stirring occasionally.
4. Top with chopped nuts and fruit.

Peanut Butter and Banana Sandwich

Ingredients:
- 2 slices of whole grain bread
- 1 tablespoon of peanut butter
- 1/2 banana, sliced

Instructions:
1. Toast the slices of bread.
2. on one slice of bread, spread the peanut butter.
3. Add the sliced banana on top.
4. Top with the other slice of bread.

Chia Seed Pudding

Ingredients:

- 1/4 cup of chia seeds
- 1 cup of almond milk
- 1/2 teaspoon of vanilla extract
- 1 tablespoon of honey
- 1/2 cup of chopped fruit (strawberries, blueberries, raspberries)

Instructions:

1. In a bowl, combine the chia seeds, almond milk, vanilla extract, and honey.
2. Stir well and let sit for 5-10 minutes.
3. Stir again and let sit in the refrigerator for about an hour, or overnight.
4. Top with chopped fruit.

Tofu and Veggie Breakfast Wrap

Ingredients:
- 1/2 block of tofu
- 1/2 onion
- 1/2 red pepper
- 1/2 teaspoon of garlic powder
- 1/2 teaspoon of onion powder
- Salt and pepper
- 1 whole wheat tortilla
- 1/2 cup of spinach

Instructions:
1. Mash the tofu with a fork.
2. Chop the onion and red pepper.
3. Heat a non-stick skillet over medium-high heat.
4. Add the onion and red.

Blueberry Oat Bran Muffins

Ingredients:
- 1 cup of oat bran
- 1/2 cup of whole wheat flour
- 1/2 cup of almond milk
- 1/2 cup of unsweetened applesauce
- 1/4 cup of maple syrup
- 1 teaspoon of baking powder
- 1/2 teaspoon of cinnamon
- 1/2 cup of blueberries

Instructions:
1. Preheat the oven to 375°F (190°C) and line a muffin tin with paper liners.
2. In a bowl, mix together the oat bran, whole wheat flour, baking powder, and cinnamon.
3. In a separate bowl, whisk together the almond milk, applesauce, and maple syrup.
4. Add the wet ingredients to the dry ingredients and stir until well combined.
5. Gently fold in the blueberries.
6. Divide the batter among the muffin cups.
7. Bake for 20-25 minutes.

Banana Walnut Pancakes

Ingredients:
- 1 ripe banana
- 1/2 cup of whole wheat flour
- 1/2 cup of almond milk
- 1 egg
- 1 tablespoon of baking powder
- 1/4 cup of chopped walnuts

Instructions:
1. Mash the banana in a bowl.
2. Add the whole wheat flour, almond milk, egg, and baking powder.
3. Mix well.
4. Heat a non-stick skillet over medium-high heat.
5. Pour ¼ cup of the batter on top of the skillet for each pancake.
6. Sprinkle chopped walnuts on top of each pancake.
7. Cook for 2-3 minutes on each side or until golden brown.

Vegetable Frittata

Ingredients:
- 1/2 onion, chopped
- 1/2 red pepper, chopped
- 1/2 cup of chopped spinach
- 4 eggs
- 1/4 cup of almond milk
- 1/4 cup of shredded cheese
- Salt and pepper

Instructions:
1. Preheat the oven to 375°F (190°C).
2. Heat a non-stick skillet over medium-high heat.
3. Add the onion and red pepper to the skillet and sauté for 3-4 minutes.
4. Add the chopped spinach and sauté for an additional minute.
5. In a bowl, mix together the almond milk, eggs, salt, and pepper.
6. Pour the egg mixture into the skillet.
7. Cook for 2-3 minutes or until the edges start to set.
8. Sprinkle shredded cheese on top.
9. Place the skillet in the oven and bake for 10-15 minutes or until the center is set.

Quinoa Breakfast Bowl

Ingredients:

- 1 cup of cooked quinoa
- 1/2 cup of chopped fruit (apple, banana, berries)
- 1/4 cup of chopped nuts (almonds, walnuts, pecans)
- 1 tablespoon of honey

Instructions:

1. In a bowl, combine the cooked quinoa, chopped fruit, and chopped nuts.
2. Drizzle honey on top.

Lunch Recipes

Chickpea Salad

Ingredients:

- 1 can chickpeas, drained and rinsed
- 1 small red onion, chopped
- 1 red bell pepper, chopped
- 1/2 cucumber, chopped
- 2 tbsp lemon juice
- 2 tbsp olive oil
- 1 tsp dried oregano
- Salt and pepper to taste

Instructions:

1. In a bowl, mix together chickpeas, red onion, red bell pepper, and cucumber.
2. In a small bowl, whisk together lemon juice, olive oil, dried oregano, salt, and pepper.
3. Pour the dressing over the chickpea salad and toss to combine.

Vegetable Stir Fry

Ingredients:
- 2 cups mixed vegetables (such as broccoli, bell peppers, carrots, and onions)
- 1 tbsp olive oil
- 1 garlic clove, minced
- 1/4 cup low-sodium soy sauce
- 1/4 cup water
- 1 tsp cornstarch

Instructions:
1. Heat the olive oil in a large skillet over medium-high heat.
2. Add the garlic and sauté for 1-2 minutes.
3. Add the mixed vegetables and sauté for 5-7 minutes, or until they are tender-crisp.
4. In a small bowl, whisk together soy sauce, water, and cornstarch.
5. Pour the sauce over the vegetables and stir until the sauce thickens.

Lentil Soup

Ingredients:
- 1 cup lentils, rinsed and drained
- 1 onion, chopped
- 2 garlic cloves, minced
- 2 carrots, chopped
- 2 celery stalks, chopped
- 4 cups vegetable broth
- 1 tsp ground cumin
- Salt and pepper to taste

Instructions:
1. In a large pot, sauté onion and garlic over medium heat until softened.
2. Add carrots and celery and continue sautéing for 5 minutes.
3. Add lentils, vegetable broth, cumin, salt, and pepper.
4. Bring to a boil, then reduce heat and simmer for 30-40 minutes, or until lentils are tender.

Black Bean Salad

Ingredients:

- 2 cups cooked black beans, drained and rinsed
- 1 red bell pepper, chopped
- 1 small red onion, chopped
- 1 jalapeño pepper, seeded and finely chopped
- 2 tbsp lime juice
- 2 tbsp olive oil
- 1 tsp ground cumin
- Salt and pepper to taste

Instructions:

1. In a large bowl, mix together black beans, red bell pepper, red onion, and jalapeño pepper.
2. In a small bowl, whisk together lime juice, olive oil, cumin, salt, and pepper.
3. Pour the dressing over the black bean salad and toss to combine.

Grilled Vegetable Wrap

Ingredients:
- 2 whole wheat tortillas
- 1 red bell pepper, sliced
- 1 yellow squash, sliced
- 1 zucchini, sliced
- 1 onion, sliced
- 2 tbsp olive oil
- Salt and pepper to taste
- 1/4 cup hummus

Instructions:
1. Preheat the grill pan to medium-high heat.
2. Toss the sliced vegetables with olive oil, salt, and pepper.
3. Grill the vegetables until tender and slightly charred, about 10-12 minutes.
4. Spread the hummus on the tortillas, then add the grilled vegetables.

Quinoa Salad

Ingredients:

- 1 cup cooked quinoa
- 1/2 cup canned chickpeas, drained and rinsed
- 1 small cucumber, chopped
- 1 small red onion, chopped
- 1/4 cup chopped fresh parsley
- 2 tbsp lemon juice
- 2 tbsp olive oil
- Salt and pepper to taste

Instructions:

1. In a large bowl, mix together quinoa, chickpeas, cucumber, red onion, and parsley.
2. In a smaller bowl, mix together lemon juice, olive oil, salt, and pepper.
3. Pour the dressing over the quinoa salad and toss to combine.

Tofu Stir Fry

Ingredients:

- 1 block extra firm tofu, cubed
- 2 cups mixed vegetables (such as broccoli, bell peppers, carrots, and onions)
- 1 tbsp olive oil
- 1 garlic clove, minced
- 1/4 cup low-sodium soy sauce
- 1/4 cup water
- 1 tsp cornstarch

Instructions:

1. Heat the olive oil in a large skillet over medium-high heat.
2. Add the garlic and sauté for 1-2 minutes.
3. Add the tofu and sauté for 5-7 minutes, or until lightly browned.
4. Add the mixed vegetables and continue sautéing for another 5-7 minutes, or until they are tender-crisp.
5. In a small bowl, whisk together soy sauce, water, and cornstarch.
6. Pour the sauce over the tofu and vegetables and stir until the sauce thickens.

Chickpea Curry

Ingredients:

- 1 can chickpeas, drained and rinsed
- 1 onion, chopped
- 2 garlic cloves, minced
- 1 tbsp grated fresh ginger
- 1 can diced tomatoes
- 1 tsp ground cumin
- 1 tsp ground coriander
- 1/2 tsp turmeric
- Salt and pepper to taste

Instructions:

1. In a large pot, sauté onion, garlic, and ginger over medium heat until softened.
2. Add diced tomatoes, chickpeas, cumin, coriander, turmeric, salt, and pepper.
3. Bring to a boil, then reduce heat and simmer for 20-25 minutes, or until the curry has thickened.

Avocado and Tomato Sandwich

Ingredients:
- 2 slices whole grain bread
- 1/2 avocado, mashed
- 1 small tomato, sliced
- 1/4 cup alfalfa sprouts
- Salt and pepper to taste

Instructions:
1. Toast the bread slices.
2. Spread mashed avocado on one slice of bread.
3. Layer tomato slices and alfalfa sprouts on top of the avocado.
4. Sprinkle with salt and pepper, then top with the other slice of bread.

Dinner Recipes

Lentil and Vegetable Curry

Ingredients:
- 1 cup lentils
- 1 onion, chopped
- 2 garlic cloves, minced
- 1 tbsp grated ginger
- 1 tbsp curry powder
- 1 can diced tomatoes
- 2 cups mixed vegetables (such as carrots, cauliflower, and green beans)
- 1 cup vegetable broth
- 1 tbsp olive oil
- Salt and pepper to taste

Instructions:
1. Rinse and drain the lentils, and set aside.
2. Heat the olive oil in a large pot over medium heat.
3. Add the onion, garlic, and ginger, and sauté until softened.
4. Add the curry powder and stir for 1 minute.
5. Add the diced tomatoes, mixed vegetables, lentils, and vegetable broth.
6. Bring to a boil, then lower the heat and simmer for 20-25 minutes or until lentils and vegetables are tender.
7. Season with pepper and salt to taste.

Grilled Tofu and Vegetable Kebabs

Ingredients:
- 1 block of extra firm tofu
- 2 bell peppers, cut into chunks
- 1 zucchini, sliced
- 1 onion, cut into chunks
- 1 tbsp olive oil
- 1 tbsp balsamic vinegar
- Salt and pepper to taste

Instructions:
1. Preheat grill to medium-high heat.
2. Cut tofu into cubes and place in a large bowl.
3. Add the bell peppers, zucchini, and onion to the bowl.
4. Drizzle the olive oil and balsamic vinegar over the mixture and toss to coat.
5. Thread the vegetables and tofu onto skewers.
6. Grill the skewers for 10-15 minutes or until vegetables are tender, turning occasionally.
7. Season with salt and pepper to taste.

Cauliflower Fried Rice

Ingredients:
- 1 head cauliflower
- 1 carrot, diced
- 1 onion, diced
- 2 garlic cloves, minced
- 1 tbsp grated ginger
- 2 tbsp low-sodium soy sauce
- 1 tbsp olive oil
- 1 egg, beaten
- Salt and pepper to taste

Instructions:
1. Cut cauliflower into florets and pulse in a food processor until it resembles rice.
2. Heat the olive oil in a large skillet over medium-high heat.
3. Add the carrot, onion, garlic, and ginger, and sauté until softened.
4. Add the cauliflower rice and stir-fry for 5-7 minutes.
5. Push the rice to the side of the skillet and pour the beaten egg in the center.
6. Scramble the egg until cooked, then mix it into the rice.
7. Add the soy sauce and stir until well combined.
8. Season with pepper and salt to taste.

Spicy Sweet Potato and Black Bean Enchiladas

Ingredients:

- 4 large sweet potatoes, peeled and cubed
- 1 can black beans, rinsed and drained
- 1 onion, chopped
- 2 garlic cloves, minced
- 1 tbsp chili powder
- 1 tsp ground cumin
- 8 corn tortillas
- 1 cup enchilada sauce
- 1 cup shredded cheddar cheese
- 1 tbsp olive oil
- Salt and pepper to taste

Instructions:

1. Preheat oven to 375°F.
2. In a large skillet, heat the olive oil over medium heat.
3. Add the sweet potatoes, onion, and garlic, and sauté until sweet potatoes are tender.
4. Add the black beans, chili powder, and cumin, and stir to combine.
5. Heat the tortillas in the microwave or on a skillet for a few seconds to soften.
6. Spread a spoonful of the enchilada sauce on each tortilla.
7. Add a scoop of the sweet potato and black bean mixture to each tortilla, and roll up tightly.
8. Place the rolled tortillas in a baking dish, seam side down.

9. Pour the remaining enchilada sauce on top of the tortillas.
10. Spray the shredded cheese on top.
11. Bake in the oven for 20-25 minutes or until cheese is melted and bubbly.
12. Season with pepper and salt to taste.

Quinoa and Vegetable Stir-Fry

Ingredients:

- 1 cup quinoa
- 2 cups mixed vegetables (such as broccoli, bell peppers, and carrots)
- 1 onion, chopped
- 2 garlic cloves, minced
- 1 tbsp grated ginger
- 2 tbsp low-sodium soy sauce
- 1 tbsp olive oil
- Salt and pepper to taste

Instructions:

1. Rinse quinoa in a fine mesh strainer and cook according to package instructions.
2. Heat the olive oil in a large skillet over medium-high heat.
3. Add the onion, garlic, and ginger, and sauté until softened.
4. Add the mixed vegetables and stir-fry for 5-10 minutes or until tender.
5. Add the cooked quinoa and soy sauce, and stir until well combined.
6. Season with pepper and salt to taste.

Spinach and Feta Stuffed Portobello Mushrooms

Ingredients:
- 4 large portobello mushrooms, stems removed
- 2 cups fresh spinach
- 1/2 cup crumbled feta cheese
- 1/4 cup chopped sun-dried tomatoes
- 2 garlic cloves, minced
- 1 tbsp olive oil
- Salt and pepper to taste

Instructions:
1. Preheat oven to 375°F.
2. Brush the portobello mushrooms with olive oil and place them on a baking sheet, gill side up.
3. In a large skillet, heat the olive oil over medium heat.
4. Add the spinach and garlic, and sauté until spinach is wilted.
5. Add the feta cheese and sun-dried tomatoes, and stir until well combined.
6. Divide the spinach mixture evenly among the mushroom caps.
7. Bake in the oven for 20-25 minutes or until mushrooms are tender.
8. Season with salt and pepper to taste.

Chickpea and Vegetable Tagine

Ingredients:
- 1 onion, chopped
- 2 garlic cloves, minced
- 1 tbsp grated ginger
- 1 tsp ground cinnamon
- 1 tsp ground cumin
- 1 can chickpeas, rinsed and drained
- 2 cups mixed vegetables (such as carrots, zucchini, and bell peppers)
- 1 cup vegetable broth
- 2 tbsp chopped fresh cilantro
- 1 tbsp olive oil
- Salt and pepper to taste

Instructions:
1. Heat the olive oil in a large pot over medium heat.
2. Add the onion, garlic, and ginger, and sauté until softened.
3. Add the cumin and cinnamon, and stir for 1 minute.
4. Add the chickpeas, mixed vegetables, and vegetable broth.
5. Bring to a boil, then reduce heat and simmer for 20-25 minutes or until vegetables are tender.
6. Stir in the chopped

Zucchini Noodles with Tomato and Basil

Ingredients:
- 4 medium zucchini, spiralized
- 1 onion, chopped
- 2 garlic cloves, minced
- 2 cups diced tomatoes
- 1/4 cup chopped fresh basil
- 1 tbsp olive oil
- Salt and pepper to taste

Instructions:
1. Heat the olive oil in a large skillet over medium heat.
2. Add the onion and garlic, and sauté until softened.
3. Add the diced tomatoes and simmer for 5-7 minutes.
4. Add the zucchini noodles and stir until well combined.
5. Cook until zucchini is tender, for about 3-5 minutes.
6. Stir in the chopped basil.
7. Season with pepper and salt to taste.

Roasted Vegetable and Quinoa Salad

Ingredients:

- 1 cup quinoa
- 2 cups mixed vegetables (such as sweet potatoes, broccoli, and bell peppers)
- 2 garlic cloves, minced
- 1 tbsp olive oil
- 1/4 cup chopped fresh parsley
- 1/4 cup crumbled feta cheese
- Salt and pepper to taste

Instructions:

1. Preheat oven to 400°F.
2. Toss mixed vegetables and garlic with olive oil, and spread on a baking sheet.
3. Roast in the oven for 20-25 minutes or until vegetables are tender.
4. In a large bowl, combine cooked quinoa and roasted vegetables.
5. Stir in chopped parsley and crumbled feta cheese.
6. Season with pepper and salt to taste.

Snacks Recipes

Roasted Chickpeas

Ingredients:

- 2 cans (15 oz each) chickpeas, rinsed and drained
- 2 tablespoons olive oil
- 1 teaspoon garlic powder
- 1 teaspoon smoked paprika
- 1/2 teaspoon salt
- 1/4 teaspoon black pepper

Instructions:

1. Preheat the oven to 400°F (200°C).
2. Rinse and drain the chickpeas and use paper towels pat them dry.
3. In a bowl, toss the chickpeas with the olive oil, garlic powder, smoked paprika, salt, and pepper until they are evenly coated.
4. Spread the chickpeas out in a single layer on a baking sheet.
5. Bake for 20-30 minutes, shaking the pan occasionally, until the chickpeas are crispy and golden brown.
6. Let the chickpeas cool for a few minutes before serving.

Nutritional information per serving (1/2 cup)
Calories: 140, Protein: 6g, Fat: 6g, Carbohydrates: 16g, Fiber: 5g, Sugar: 0g, Sodium: 230mg

Veggie and Hummus Wraps

Ingredients:
- 4 whole wheat tortillas
- 1/2 cup hummus
- 2 cups mixed veggies (such as sliced bell peppers, cucumbers, carrots, and spinach)
- 1/4 cup crumbled feta cheese
- 1 tablespoon olive oil
- Salt and pepper to taste

Instructions:
1. Heat the tortillas in the microwave for 10-20 seconds to make them easier to roll.
2. Spread 2 tablespoons of hummus on each tortilla, leaving a small border around the edges.
3. Layer the veggies and feta cheese on top of the hummus.
1. 4   Drizzle a little olive oil over the veggies, then sprinkle with salt and pepper.
4. Roll up the tortillas tightly, tucking in the ends as you go.
5. Slice each wrap in half diagonally and serve immediately.

Nutritional information per serving (1 wrap)
Calories: 340, Protein: 11g, Fat: 16g, Carbohydrates: 38g, Fiber: 8g, Sugar: 5g, Sodium: 730mg

Baked Sweet Potato Fries

Ingredients:

- 2 large sweet potatoes
- 2 tablespoons olive oil
- 1 teaspoon garlic powder
- 1/2 teaspoon paprika
- Salt and pepper to taste

Instructions:

1. Preheat the oven to 425°F (218°C).
2. Peel the sweet potatoes and cut them into thin, even strips.
3. In a large bowl, toss the sweet potato strips with the olive oil, garlic powder, paprika, salt, and pepper until they are evenly coated.
4. Bring out the sweet potato strips in a single layer on a baking sheet lined with parchment paper.
5. Bake for 20-25 minutes, flipping the fries over halfway through, until they are crispy and lightly browned.
6. Serve immediately with your preferred dipping sauce.

Nutritional information per serving (1/2 cup)

Calories: 130, Protein: 1g, Fat: 6g, Carbohydrates: 19g, Fiber: 3g, Sugar: 5g, Sodium: 170mg

Caprese Salad Skewers

Ingredients:
- 1 pint cherry tomatoes
- 8 oz fresh mozzarella cheese, cut into small cubes
- 1/4 cup fresh basil leaves
- 2 tablespoons balsamic glaze
- Salt and pepper to taste
- Skewers (wooden or metal)

Instructions:
1. Rinse the cherry tomatoes and pat them dry.
2. Thread one cherry tomato, one cube of mozzarella, and one basil leaf onto each skewer, repeating until all the ingredients are used up.
3. Arrange the skewers on a serving platter.
4. Drizzle the balsamic glaze over the skewers, then sprinkle with salt and pepper to taste.
5. Serve immediately, or refrigerate until ready to serve.

Nutritional information per serving (2 skewers)
Calories: 140, Protein: 10g, Fat: 8g, Carbohydrates: 7g, Fiber: 1g, Sugar: 4g, Sodium: 290mg

Spicy Edamame

Ingredients:
- 1 lb frozen edamame pods, thawed
- 2 tablespoons soy sauce
- 1 tablespoon sesame oil
- 1 tablespoon sriracha sauce
- 1 teaspoon garlic powder
- Salt to taste

Instructions:
1. Cook the edamame pods according to the package instructions, then drain them and set aside.
2. In a small bowl, whisk together the soy sauce, sesame oil, sriracha sauce, garlic powder, and salt until well combined.
3. Toss the edamame pods with the spicy sauce until they are evenly coated.
4. Serve immediately as a snack or appetizer.

Nutritional information per serving (1/4 of the recipe):

Calories: 170, Protein: 12g, Fat: 7g, Carbohydrates: 15g, Fiber: 7g, Sugar: 2g, Sodium: 710mg

Salads and Bowls for Vegetarian

Kale and Brussels Sprouts Salad with Lemon Vinaigrette

Ingredients:
- 1 bunch kale, stemmed and chopped
- 1 pound Brussels sprouts, trimmed and thinly sliced
- 1/2 cup slivered almonds
- 1/2 cup dried cranberries
- 1/2 cup grated Parmesan cheese

For the Lemon Vinaigrette:
- 1/4 cup freshly squeezed lemon juice
- 1/4 cup olive oil
- 1 teaspoon Dijon mustard
- 1 clove garlic, minced
- Salt and freshly ground black pepper, to taste

Instructions:
1. In a large bowl, combine the chopped kale and sliced Brussels sprouts. Toss to combine.
2. In a small bowl, whisk together the lemon juice, olive oil, Dijon mustard, minced garlic, salt, and black pepper to make the vinaigrette.
3. Pour the vinaigrette over the kale and Brussels sprouts, and toss to coat well.
4. Add the slivered almonds, dried cranberries, and grated Parmesan cheese to the salad, and toss to combine.
5. Serve immediately, or refrigerate until ready to serve.

Nutrition Information (per serving)
Calories: 300 Protein: 12g Fat: 20g Carbohydrates: 27g Fiber: 7g Sugar: 13g Sodium: 380mg

Quinoa and Black Bean Salad

Ingredients:
- 1 cup uncooked quinoa
- 1 can (15 oz) black beans, rinsed and drained
- 1 red bell pepper, diced
- 1/2 red onion, diced
- 1/2 cup chopped fresh cilantro
- 1 avocado, diced
- 1 jalapeno pepper, seeded and finely chopped (optional)

For the Dressing:
- 1/4 cup freshly squeezed lime juice
- 1/4 cup olive oil
- 1 teaspoon honey
- 1/2 teaspoon ground cumin
- Salt and freshly ground black pepper, to taste

Instructions:
1. Rinse the quinoa in a fine-mesh strainer and place it in a medium saucepan with 2 cups of water. Bring the water to a boil, then lower the heat and cover the saucepan. Cook the quinoa until all the water evaporates, about 15 minutes.
2. Combine the cooked quinoa in a large bowl, black beans, diced red bell pepper, diced red onion, chopped cilantro, diced avocado, and chopped jalapeno pepper (if using).
3. In a small bowl, mix together the olive oil, lime juice, honey, ground cumin, salt, and black pepper to make the dressing.

4. Pour the dressing over the quinoa and black bean mixture, and toss to coat well.
5. Serve immediately, or keep chill until ready to serve.

Nutrition Information (per serving)

Calories: 385 Protein: 12g Fat: 19g Carbohydrates: 46g Fiber: 13g Sugar: 5g Sodium: 290mg

Roasted Beet and Goat Cheese Salad

Ingredients:
- 4 medium beets, trimmed and peeled
- 4 cups mixed greens
- 1/2 cup crumbled goat cheese
- 1/4 cup chopped walnuts
- 2 tablespoons balsamic vinegar
- 2 tablespoons olive oil
- Salt and freshly ground black pepper, to taste

Instructions:
1. Preheat the oven to 400°F. Wrap each beet in aluminum foil and place them on a baking sheet. Roast the beets until they are soft when pierced with a fork, for about 45 minutes, depending on their size. Once they are done, remove from the oven and allow them to cool.
2. Once the beets are cooled, slice them into thin wedges or rounds and set aside.
3. In a large bowl, combine the mixed greens, crumbled goat cheese, and chopped walnuts.
4. In a bowl, whisk together the balsamic vinegar, olive oil, salt, and black pepper to make the dressing.
5. Add the roasted beets to the salad, and toss to combine.
6. Drizzle the dressing over the salad, and toss again to coat everything evenly.
7. Serve immediately, garnished with additional chopped walnuts and goat cheese, if desired.

Nutrition Information (per serving)

Calories: 195 Protein: 6g Fat: 12g Carbohydrates: 18g Fiber: 5g Sugar: 12g Sodium: 215mg

Buddha Bowls with Tahini Dressing

Ingredients:

For the Buddha Bowls
- 1 cup uncooked quinoa
- 1 can (15 oz) chickpeas, rinsed and drained
- 2 cups chopped kale
- 2 cups chopped sweet potatoes
- 2 cups chopped broccoli
- 2 tablespoons olive oil
- Salt and freshly ground black pepper, to taste

For the Tahini Dressing:
- 1/4 cup tahini
- 1/4 cup freshly squeezed lemon juice
- 2 tablespoons olive oil
- 2 tablespoons honey
- 1 clove garlic, minced
- Salt and freshly ground black pepper, to taste

Instructions:
1. Rinse the quinoa in a fine-mesh strainer and place it in a medium saucepan with 2 cups of water. Bring the water to a boil, then lower the heat and cover the saucepan. Cook the quinoa until all the water has been absorbed, about 15 minutes.
2. Preheat the oven to 400°F. On a baking sheet, toss the chickpeas, chopped kale, chopped sweet potatoes, and chopped broccoli with olive oil, salt, and black pepper.

Roast in the oven until the vegetables are tender, about 20-25 minutes.
3. Whisk together In a bowl, the tahini, lemon juice, olive oil, honey, minced garlic, salt, and black pepper to make the dressing.
4. Divide the cooked quinoa and roasted vegetables evenly among four bowls.
5. Drizzle the tahini dressing over the bowls and serve.

Nutrition Information (per serving)

Calories: 460 Protein: 14g Fat: 21g Carbohydrates: 60g Fiber: 12g Sugar: 16g Sodium: 310mg

Mediterranean Grain Bowl

Ingredients:

For the Grain Bowl
- 1 cup uncooked farro
- 1 can (15 oz) chickpeas, rinsed and drained
- 2 cups chopped cucumber
- 2 cups cherry tomatoes, halved
- 1 cup crumbled feta cheese
- 1/4 cup chopped fresh parsley
- 1/4 cup chopped fresh mint
- 1/4 cup sliced kalamata olives
- 2 tablespoons olive oil
- Salt and freshly ground black pepper, to taste

For the Lemon Garlic Dressing:
- 1/4 cup freshly squeezed lemon juice
- 2 cloves garlic, minced
- 2 tablespoons olive oil
- 1 tablespoon honey
- Salt and freshly ground black pepper, to taste

Instructions:
1. Rinse the farro in a fine-mesh strainer and place it in a medium saucepan with 3 cups of water. Bring the water to a boil, then reduce the heat to low and cover the saucepan. Cook the farro until all the water has been absorbed, about 30 minutes.
2. Combine in an outsized bowl, the chickpeas, cooked farro, chopped cucumber, halved cherry tomatoes, crumbled feta

cheese, chopped fresh parsley, chopped fresh mint, and sliced kalamata olives.
3. In a bowl, whisk together the lemon juice, minced garlic, olive oil, honey, salt, and black pepper to make the dressing.
4. Drizzle the dressing over the grain bowl and toss everything to combine.
5. Garnished with extra chopped fresh herbs, if desired and serve immediately.

Nutrition Information (per serving)

Calories: 530 Protein: 18g Fat: 23g Carbohydrates: 65g Fiber: 13g Sugar: 12g Sodium: 820mg

Vegetarian Soups and Stews

Vegetable and Lentil Soup

Ingredients:
- 1 tablespoon olive oil
- 1 onion, chopped
- 2 carrots, chopped
- 2 celery stalks, chopped
- 2 garlic cloves, minced
- 1 teaspoon dried thyme
- 1 teaspoon dried oregano
- 1 teaspoon ground cumin
- 1 teaspoon smoked paprika
- 1/2 teaspoon red pepper flakes
- 6 cups vegetable broth
- 1 can (28 oz) diced tomatoes, undrained
- 1 cup brown or green lentils, rinsed and drained
- 2 cups chopped kale
- Salt and freshly ground black pepper, to taste

Instructions:
1. Heat the olive oil in a large pot over medium heat. Add the onion, carrots, and celery and sauté until the vegetables are tender, about 5-7 minutes.
2. Add the minced garlic, dried thyme, dried oregano, ground cumin, smoked paprika, and red pepper flakes to the pot, and sauté for another 1-2 minutes until fragrant.
3. Pour the vegetable broth and diced tomatoes into the pot, and bring the soup to a boil.

4. Add the lentils to the soup, lower the heat, and simmer until the lentils are tender, about 30-35 minutes.
5. Add the chopped kale to the soup during the last 10 minutes of cooking.
6. Season the soup with salt and freshly ground black pepper to taste.
7. Ladle the soup into bowls and serve.

Nutrition Information (per serving)

Calories: 200 Protein: 10g Fat: 3g Carbohydrates: 35g Fiber: 12g Sugar: 7g Sodium: 990mg

Creamy Tomato Soup

Ingredients:
- 1 tablespoon olive oil
- 1 onion, chopped
- 2 garlic cloves, minced
- 1 can (28 oz) crushed tomatoes
- 2 cups vegetable broth
- 1/2 cup heavy cream
- 2 teaspoons dried basil
- Salt and freshly ground black pepper, to taste

Instructions:
1. Heat the olive oil in a large pot over medium heat. Add the chopped onion and sauté until the onion is translucent, about 5-7 minutes.
2. Add the minced garlic to the pot and sauté for another 1-2 minutes until fragrant.
3. Pour the can of vegetable broth and crushed tomatoes into the pot, and bring the soup to a boil.
4. Reduce the heat to low and simmer the soup for 10-15 minutes, stirring occasionally.
5. Using an immersion blender or transferring the soup to a blender, puree the soup until smooth.
6. Add the heavy cream and dried basil to the soup, and stir until the cream is fully incorporated.
7. Season the soup with salt and freshly ground black pepper to taste.
8. Ladle the soup into bowls and serve.

Nutrition Information (per serving)
Calories: 220 Protein: 4g Fat: 16g Carbohydrates: 18g Fiber: 4g Sugar: 9g Sodium: 640mg

Butternut Squash Soup

Ingredients:

- 1 medium butternut squash, peeled, seeded, and chopped into small pieces
- 1 tablespoon olive oil
- 1 onion, chopped
- 2 garlic cloves, minced
- 1 teaspoon ground cumin
- 1/2 teaspoon ground cinnamon
- 4 cups vegetable broth
- 1/4 cup heavy cream (optional)
- Salt and freshly ground black pepper, to taste

Instructions:

1. Preheat the oven to 400°F.
2. In a large bowl, toss the chopped butternut squash with the olive oil, and spread the squash out on a baking sheet.
3. Roast the squash in the oven for 20-25 minutes, or until the squash is tender and lightly browned.
4. In a large pot, sauté the chopped onion in a bit of olive oil until the onion is soft, about 5-7 minutes.
5. Add the minced garlic, ground cumin, and ground cinnamon to the pot, and sauté for another 1-2 minutes until fragrant.
6. Add the roasted butternut squash and vegetable broth to the pot, and bring the soup to a boil.
7. Reduce the heat to low, and simmer for about 10 minutes.
8. Using a transferring the soup to a blender or an immersion blender, puree the soup until smooth.

9. Stir in the heavy cream (optional), and season the soup with salt and freshly ground black pepper to taste.
10. Ladle the soup into bowls and serve.

Nutrition Information (per serving):

Calories: 180 Protein: 3g Fat: 8g Carbohydrates: 27g Fiber: 5g Sugar: 6g Sodium: 990mg

Vegetarian Chili

Ingredients:
- 1 tablespoon olive oil
- 1 onion, chopped
- 3 garlic cloves, minced
- 2 bell peppers, chopped
- 2 carrots, chopped
- 1 zucchini, chopped
- 1 can (28 oz) crushed tomatoes
- 2 cans (15 oz) kidney beans, drained and rinsed
- 1 can (15 oz) black beans, drained and rinsed
- 1 tablespoon chili powder
- 1 teaspoon ground cumin
- 1/2 teaspoon smoked paprika
- Salt and freshly ground black pepper, to taste

Optional toppings:
- Shredded cheddar cheese
- Sour cream
- Chopped cilantro

Instructions:
1. In a large pot, sauté the chopped onion in the olive oil until the onion is soft, about 57 minutes.
2. Add the minced garlic, chopped bell peppers, chopped carrots, and chopped zucchini to the pot, and sauté for another 5-7 minutes until the vegetables are slightly softened.

3. Pour the can of crushed tomatoes, drained and rinsed kidney beans, and drained and rinsed black beans into the pot, and stir to combine.
4. Add the chili powder, ground cumin, smoked paprika, salt, and freshly ground black pepper to the pot, and stir to combine.
5. Bring the chili to a boil, then reduce the heat to low and let the chili simmer for 30-45 minutes, stirring occasionally.
6. Ladle the chili into bowls, and top with shredded cheddar cheese, a dollop of sour cream, and chopped cilantro, if desired.

Nutrition Information (per serving)

Calories: 270 Protein: 13g Fat: 4g Carbohydrates: 50g Fiber: 17g Sugar: 11g Sodium: 750mg

Spicy Soba Noodle Soup

Ingredients:
- 6 cups vegetable broth
- 1 tablespoon sesame oil
- 1 tablespoon grated ginger
- 3 garlic cloves, minced
- 2 tablespoons soy sauce
- 2 tablespoons rice vinegar
- 2 tablespoons chili paste
- 1 tablespoon honey
- 8 oz. soba noodles
- 4 cups chopped bok choy
- 1 cup sliced shiitake mushrooms
- 1 cup sliced scallions
- 1 cup chopped cilantro
- Lime wedges, for serving

Instructions:
1. In a large pot, bring the vegetable broth to a boil.
2. Reduce the heat to low, and add the sesame oil, grated ginger, minced garlic, soy sauce, rice vinegar, chili paste, and honey to the pot.
3. Stir the ingredients together, and let the broth simmer for 10-15 minutes.
4. Cook the soba noodles according to the package instructions, and drain them when they are done.
5. Add the chopped bok choy and sliced shiitake mushrooms to the pot, and let them cook for 5-7 minutes, or until the vegetables are tender.

6. Add the cooked soba noodles and sliced scallions to the pot, and let everything cook together for another 2-3 minutes.
7. Ladle the soup into plates, and decorate with chopped cilantro and lime wedges.

Nutrition Information (per serving)

Calories: 280 Protein: 11g Fat: 4g Carbohydrates: 56g Fiber: 4g Sugar: 11g Sodium: 1900mg

Roasted Chickpeas

Ingredients:
- 1 can chickpeas, drained and rinsed
- 1 tbsp olive oil
- 1 tsp garlic powder
- 1 tsp paprika
- Salt and pepper to taste

Instructions:
1. Preheat oven to 400°F.
2. Pat chickpeas use paper towel to dry.
3. Toss chickpeas with olive oil, garlic powder, paprika, salt, and pepper.
4. Spread on a baking sheet and roast in the oven for 20-25 minutes or until crispy.

Guacamole with Veggie Sticks

Ingredients:
- 2 ripe avocados
- 1 small onion, chopped
- 1 garlic clove, minced
- 1 tbsp lime juice
- Salt and pepper to taste
- Veggie sticks (such as carrots, celery, and bell peppers) for dipping

Instructions:
1. Cut avocados in half and get rid of the pit.
2. Scrape the flesh into a bowl and mash with a fork.
3. Add onion, garlic, lime juice, salt, and pepper, and stir until well combined.
4. Serve with veggie sticks for dipping.

Hummus and Pita Chips

Ingredients:
- 1 can chickpeas, drained and rinsed
- 1/4 cup tahini
- 1/4 cup lemon juice
- 2 garlic cloves, minced
- 2 tbsp olive oil
- Salt and pepper to taste
- Pita bread, cut into triangles

Instructions:
1. In a food processor, combine chickpeas, tahini, garlic, lemon juice, olive oil, salt, and pepper.
2. Pulse until smooth.
3. Serve with pita chips for dipping.

Greek Yogurt and Fruit Parfait

Ingredients:
- 1 cup Greek yogurt
- 1 cup mixed berries (such as strawberries, blueberries, and raspberries)
- 1/4 cup granola
- 1 tbsp honey

Instructions:
1. In a small bowl, layer Greek yogurt, mixed berries, and granola.
2. Drizzle with honey.

Caprese Skewers

Ingredients:
- Cherry tomatoes
- Fresh basil leaves
- Fresh mozzarella cheese, cut into cubes
- Balsamic vinegar

Instructions:
1. Thread cherry tomatoes, mozzarella cheese cubes, and basil leaves, onto skewers.
2. Drizzle with balsamic vinegar.

Veggie Roll-Ups

Ingredients:
- 1 large flour tortilla
- 2 bsp cream cheese
- 1/2 cup mixed vegetables (such as carrots, cucumber, and bell peppers), julienned

Instructions:
1. Spread cream cheese on tortilla.
2. Layer mixed vegetables on top.
3. Roll up tortilla tightly and slice into rounds.

Roasted Almonds

Ingredients:
- 1 cup raw almonds
- 1 tbsp olive oil
- Salt to taste

Instructions:
1. Preheat oven to 350°F.
2. Toss almonds with olive oil and salt.
3. Spread on a baking sheet and roast.

No-Sugar chocolate chip cookies

Ingredients:

1 cup almond flour

1/4 cup sugar-free chocolate chips

1/4 cup unsweetened applesauce

1/4 cup coconut oil

1/4 tsp baking powder

1/4 tsp salt

Instructions:
1. Preheat the oven to 350°F and line a baking sheet with parchment paper.
2. Combine almond flour, sugar-free chocolate chips, baking powder, and salt In a mixing bowl.
3. Add applesauce and coconut oil to the bowl and mix until the dough forms.
4. Scoop the dough with a spoon and shape it into small balls.

5. Place the dough balls on the baking sheet and flatten them slightly with a fork.
6. Bake the cookies for 15 minutes or until they turn golden brown.
7. Remove from oven and allow to cool for 5 minutes before serving.

Desert Recipes

Vegan Banana Pudding

Ingredients:

- 2 ripe bananas
- 1/4 cup almond milk
- 1/4 cup cornstarch
- 1/4 cup maple syrup
- 1/4 tsp vanilla extract

Instructions:

1. In a blender, puree bananas and almond milk until smooth.
2. In a saucepan, combine cornstarch, maple syrup, and vanilla extract.
3. Gradually add banana puree to the saucepan, whisking continuously until it thickens.
4. Remove from heat and let it cool down.
5. Serve in a bowl and garnish with banana slices.

Apple Cinnamon Baked Oatmeal

Ingredients:

- 1 cup rolled oats
- 1/2 cup unsweetened applesauce
- 1/2 cup almond milk
- 1/4 cup maple syrup
- 1 tsp cinnamon
- 1 apple, peeled and diced

Instructions:

1. Preheat oven to 350°F.
2. In a mixing bowl, combine oats, applesauce, almond milk, maple syrup, and cinnamon.
3. Stir in diced apples.
4. Pour mixture into a baking dish and bake for 30 minutes or until golden brown.
5. Remove from oven and let it cool before serving.

Vegan Chocolate Avocado Mousse

Ingredients:

- 2 ripe avocados
- 1/4 cup unsweetened cocoa powder
- 1/4 cup maple syrup
- 1 tsp vanilla extract

Instructions:

1. In a blender, puree avocados until smooth.
2. Add cocoa powder, maple syrup, and vanilla extract to the blender and blend until creamy.
3. Chill in the refrigerator for 1 hour before serving.
4. Serve with fresh berries.

Sugar-free Blueberry Sorbet

Ingredients:

- 2 cups frozen blueberries
- 1/2 cup water
- 1/4 cup lemon juice
- 2 tbsp stevia

Instructions:

1. In a blender, puree frozen blueberries, water, lemon juice, and stevia until smooth.
2. Pour mixture into a container and freeze for at least 4 hours.
3. Remove from freezer and let it soften before serving.

Vegetarian Peanut Butter

Ingredients:

- 1/4 cup peanut butter
- 1/4 cup coconut oil
- 1/4 cup unsweetened cocoa powder
- 2 tbsp maple syrup
- 1/2 tsp vanilla extract

Instructions:

1. In a saucepan, melt coconut oil and peanut butter together.
2. Add maple syrup, cocoa powder, and vanilla extract to the saucepan and stir until smooth.
3. Pour mixture into a muffin tin lined with muffin cups.
4. Freeze for at least 2 hours before serving.

Sugar-free Chia Seed Pudding

Ingredients:

- 1/4 cup chia seeds
- 1 cup unsweetened almond milk
- 1/4 cup stevia
- 1 tsp vanilla extract

Instructions:

1. In a mixing bowl, combine chia seeds, almond milk, stevia, and vanilla extract.
2. Stir well and chill for about 2 hours or until it thickens.
3. Serve in a bowl with fresh berries on top.

Vegan Pumpkin Pie

Ingredients:
- 1 pre-made pie crust
- 1 can of pumpkin puree
- 1/2 cup unsweetened almond milk
- 1/4 cup maple syrup
- 1 tsp pumpkin pie spice
- 1 tsp vanilla extract

Instructions:
1. Preheat oven to 350°F.
2. In a mixing bowl, combine pumpkin puree, almond milk, maple syrup, pumpkin pie spice, and vanilla extract.
3. Pour mixture into the pie crust.
4. Bake for 45-50 minutes or until the center is set.
5. Remove from oven and let it cool before serving.

Sugar-free Coconut Macaroons

Ingredients:

- 2 cups unsweetened shredded coconut
- 1/4 cup coconut flour
- 1/4 cup coconut oil
- 1/4 cup stevia
- 1/4 cup unsweetened almond milk
- 1 tsp vanilla extract

Instructions:

1. Preheat oven to 350°F and line the parchment paper on a baking sheet.
2. In a mixing bowl, combine shredded coconut, coconut flour, stevia, and vanilla extract.
3. Add coconut oil and almond milk to the bowl and mix until the dough forms.
4. Scoop the dough with a spoon and shape it into small balls.
5. Place the dough balls on the baking sheet and bake for 15-20 minutes or until golden brown.
6. Remove from oven and let them cool before serving.

Sugar-free Apple Crumble

Ingredients:

- 4 apples, peeled and sliced
- 1 cup almond flour
- 1/4 cup coconut oil
- 1/4 cup stevia
- 1 tsp cinnamon
- 1/4 tsp nutmeg
- 1/4 tsp salt

Instructions:

1. Preheat oven to 370°F and evenly apply grease on a baking dish.
2. In a mixing bowl, combine almond flour, coconut oil, stevia, cinnamon, nutmeg, and salt. Mix until crumbly.
3. Spread the sliced apples evenly in the baking dish.
4. Sprinkle the almond flour mixture on top of the apples.
5. Bake for 30-40 minutes or until the topping is golden brown and the apples are tender.
6. Remove from oven and let it cool for a few minutes before serving. Enjoy!

High-Protein Vegetarian Recipes

Spicy Black Bean and Quinoa Bowl

Ingredients:
- 1 cup quinoa
- 1 can black beans, drained and rinsed
- 1 red bell pepper, diced
- 1 small red onion, diced
- 1 jalapeño pepper, seeded and minced
- 2 cloves garlic, minced
- 1 teaspoon ground cumin
- 1 teaspoon smoked paprika
- 1/2 teaspoon chili powder
- 1/4 teaspoon cayenne pepper
- 1 tablespoon olive oil
- Salt and black pepper to taste
- 1 lime, juiced
- 2 tablespoons chopped fresh cilantro

Instructions:
1. Rinse the quinoa thoroughly in a fine-mesh strainer and transfer it to a medium-sized saucepan. Add 2 cups of water and a pinch of salt, and bring to a boil over medium high heat. Reduce the heat to low, cover the saucepan, and simmer for 15-20 minutes, until the quinoa is tender and the water has been absorbed.
2. While the quinoa is cooking, heat the olive oil in a large skillet over medium heat. Add the red onion and red bell pepper, and sauté for 3-4 minutes, until they start to soften.

3. Add the garlic, jalapeño pepper, cumin, smoked paprika, chili powder, and cayenne pepper to the skillet, and cook for another minute or two, stirring frequently.
4. To the skillet, add the black beans and stir to combine. Cook for 5-6 minutes, until the beans are heated through.
5. Season the black bean mixture with salt and black pepper to taste. Remove the skillet from the heat and stir in the lime juice and chopped cilantro.
6. To serve, divide the quinoa among four bowls and top each with a generous scoop of the black bean mixture.

Nutritional information (per serving, based on 4 servings)
Calories: 308 Total fat: 7.7g Saturated fat: 1g Cholesterol: 0mg Sodium: 203mg Total carbohydrate: 49.2g Dietary fiber: 11.6g Sugars: 4.2g Protein: 11.6g

Lentil and Mushroom Bolognese

Ingredients:

- 1 cup brown or green lentils
- 2 tablespoons olive oil
- 1 onion, finely chopped
- 3 garlic cloves, minced
- 1 carrot, finely chopped
- 1 celery stalk, finely chopped
- 8 oz cremini mushrooms, chopped
- 1 tablespoon tomato paste
- 1 (14 oz) can diced tomatoes
- 1 cup vegetable broth
- 1 teaspoon dried oregano
- 1/2 teaspoon dried basil
- 1/2 teaspoon dried thyme
- Salt and pepper to taste
- 8 oz spaghetti or pasta of choice
- Fresh parsley, chopped (optional)

Instructions:

1. Rinse the lentils thoroughly in a fine-mesh strainer and transfer them to a large saucepan. Add 2 cups of water and a pinch of salt, and bring to a boil over medium high heat. Lower the heat, cover the saucepan, and simmer until the lentils are tender but not mushy.
2. While the lentils are cooking, heat the olive oil in a large skillet over medium heat. Add the onion, garlic, carrot, and celery, and sauté for 5-7 minutes, until the vegetables are soft and fragrant.

3. Add the mushrooms to the skillet and cook for another 5-7 minutes, until they release their liquid and start to brown.
4. Stir in the diced tomatoes, tomato paste, vegetable broth, oregano, basil, and thyme. Bring the mixture to a simmer and cook for 10-15 minutes, until the sauce thickens.
5. Once the lentils are cooked, drain any excess water and add them to the skillet with the sauce. Stir to combine and cook for another 5-7 minutes, until the lentils are heated through.
6. Cook the spaghetti or pasta according to the package instructions, until al dente.
7. Serve the lentil and mushroom bolognese over the cooked pasta, garnished with chopped parsley, if desired.

Nutritional information (per serving, based on 4 servings)

Calories: 421 Total fat: 9.5g Saturated fat: 1.3g Cholesterol: 0mg Sodium: 285mg Total carbohydrate: 69.2g Dietary fiber: 17.4g Sugars: 8.1g Protein: 18.4g

Chickpea and Spinach Curry

Ingredients:
- 1 tablespoon vegetable oil
- 1 onion, chopped
- 3 garlic cloves, minced
- 1 tablespoon grated ginger
- 2 teaspoons ground cumin
- 1 teaspoon ground coriander
- 1/2 teaspoon turmeric
- 1/4 teaspoon cayenne pepper
- 2 cups cooked chickpeas (or one 15-ounce can, drained and rinsed)
- 1 14-ounce can diced tomatoes
- 1/2 cup water
- 1 teaspoon salt
- 4 cups baby spinach leaves
- 1/4 cup chopped fresh cilantro (optional)
- Cooked rice, for serving

Instructions:
1. Heat the vegetable oil in a large saucepan or Dutch oven over medium heat. Add the onion and cook, stirring occasionally, until softened, about 5 minutes.
2. Add the garlic and ginger and cook for 1 minute, stirring constantly.
3. Add the cumin, coriander, cayenne pepper, and turmeric and cook for 1 minute, stirring constantly.

4. Add the chickpeas, diced tomatoes (with their juices), water, and salt. Bring to a simmer and cook, stirring occasionally, for 10 minutes.
5. Add the spinach leaves and cook until wilted, about 2 minutes.
6. Stir in the cilantro, if using. Serve over cooked rice.

Nutritional information (per serving, without rice):

Calories: 231; Protein: 9g; Fat: 8g; Carbohydrates: 33g; Fiber: 10g; Sugar: 8g; Sodium: 906mg

Tofu and Vegetable Stir Fry

Ingredients:
- 1 tablespoon vegetable oil
- 1 block (14-16 ounces) firm tofu, drained and pressed
- 1 red bell pepper, seeded and sliced
- 1 yellow bell pepper, seeded and sliced
- 1 zucchini, sliced
- 1 carrot, sliced
- 2 cloves garlic, minced
- 1 tablespoon minced ginger
- 1/4 cup soy sauce
- 2 tablespoons honey or agave nectar
- 1 tablespoon cornstarch
- 1/4 teaspoon red pepper flakes (optional)
- Cooked rice or noodles, for serving

Instructions:
1. Heat the vegetable oil in a large skillet or wok over medium-high heat.
2. Cut the tofu into bite-sized pieces and add to the skillet. Cook until golden brown on all sides, approximately 5 minutes. Remove from the skillet and set aside.
3. Add the yellow and red bell peppers, zucchini, and carrot to the skillet. Cook for 5-7 minutes, stirring occasionally, until the vegetables are crisp-tender.
4. Add the garlic and ginger and cook for 1 minute, stirring constantly.
5. In a small bowl, whisk together the soy sauce, honey or agave nectar, cornstarch, and red pepper flakes (if using).

6. Add the cooked tofu back to the skillet and pour the sauce over the vegetables and tofu. Cook for 1-2 minutes, until the sauce has thickened.
7. Serve over cooked rice or noodles.

Nutritional information (per serving, without rice or noodles)

Calories: 252; Protein: 17g; Fat: 13g; Carbohydrates: 20g; Fiber: 3g; Sugar: 13g; Sodium: 1463mg

Grilled Portobello Mushroom Burgers

Ingredients:
- 4 large portobello mushroom caps
- 1/4 cup balsamic vinegar
- 2 tablespoons olive oil
- 2 cloves garlic, minced
- 1/2 teaspoon dried basil
- 1/2 teaspoon dried oregano
- Salt and pepper, to taste
- 4 hamburger buns
- Toppings of your choice (lettuce, tomato, onion, avocado, etc.)

Instructions:
1. Preheat the grill or grill pan to medium-high heat.
2. In a small bowl, whisk together the balsamic vinegar, olive oil, garlic, basil, oregano, salt, and pepper.
3. Remove the stems from the caps of the portobello mushroom and clean the caps with a damp paper towel.
4. Brush the mushroom caps with the balsamic mixture, making sure to coat both sides.
5. Grill the mushroom caps for 4-5 minutes per side, until tender and lightly charred.
6. Toast the hamburger buns on the grill for 1-2 minutes, until lightly toasted.
7. Assemble the burgers with the grilled mushroom caps and toppings of your choice.

Nutritional information (per serving, without toppings)
Calories: 225; Protein: 6g; Fat: 8g; Carbohydrates: 33g; Fiber: 3g; Sugar: 7g; Sodium: 228mg

Low-Carb Vegetarian Recipes

Zucchini Noodles with Avocado Pesto

Ingredients:
- 4 medium zucchini
- 2 ripe avocados
- 1/4 cup fresh basil leaves
- 1/4 cup fresh parsley leaves
- 2 cloves garlic
- 2 tablespoons lemon juice
- 1/4 cup olive oil
- Salt and pepper, to taste
- Optional: grated Parmesan cheese for serving

Instructions:
1. Cut off the ends of the zucchini and use a spiralizer or vegetable peeler to create zucchini noodles. Set aside in a large bowl.
2. In a food processor or blender, combine the avocados, basil, parsley, garlic, lemon juice, olive oil, salt, and pepper. Blend until smooth and creamy.
3. Pour the avocado pesto over the zucchini noodles and toss to coat well.
4. Serve the zucchini noodles topped with grated Parmesan cheese, if desired.

Nutrition Information (per serving, recipe serves 4)
Calories: 328, Protein: 6g, Fat: 30g, Carbohydrates: 16g, Fiber: 8g, Sugar: 6g, Sodium: 35mg

Broccoli and Cheddar Soup

Ingredients:
- 4 cups broccoli florets
- 1 onion, chopped
- 2 cloves garlic, minced
- 4 cups vegetable or chicken broth
- 1 cup heavy cream
- 2 cups shredded cheddar cheese
- 2 tablespoons butter
- Salt and pepper, to taste

Instructions:
1. In a large pot or Dutch oven, melt the butter over medium heat. Add the onion and garlic and cook until the onion is translucent, about 5 minutes.
2. Add the broccoli florets and broth to the pot. Bring to a boil, then reduce the heat to low and simmer until the broccoli is tender, about 10-15 minutes.
3. Use an immersion blender or transfer the soup to a blender and puree until smooth.
4. Add the heavy cream and shredded cheddar cheese to the pot and stir until the cheese is melted and the soup is creamy.
5. Season the soup with salt and pepper, to taste.
6. Serve the soup hot, garnished with additional shredded cheddar cheese and chopped fresh herbs, if desired.

Nutrition Information (per serving, recipe serves 6)
Calories: 356, Protein: 14g, Fat: 28g, Carbohydrates: 13g, Fiber: 3g, Sugar: 5g, Sodium: 959mg

Roasted Brussels Sprouts with Tahini Sauce

Ingredients:
- 1 lb Brussels sprouts, trimmed and halved
- 1 tablespoon olive oil
- Salt and pepper, to taste
- 1/4 cup tahini
- 2 tablespoons lemon juice
- 2 cloves garlic, minced
- 2-4 tablespoons water, as needed
- Optional: chopped fresh herbs or sesame seeds for garnish

Instructions:
1. Preheat the oven to 400°F (200°C).
2. Toss the Brussels sprouts with olive oil, pepper, and salt. Spread them out on a baking sheet lined with parchment paper.
3. Roast the Brussels sprouts in the preheated oven until they are tender and golden brown.
4. While the Brussels sprouts are roasting, make the tahini sauce. In a small bowl, whisk together the lemon juice, tahini, garlic, and enough water to thin the sauce to your desired consistency.
5. When the Brussels sprouts are done, transfer them to a serving dish and drizzle the tahini sauce over the top.
6. Garnish with chopped fresh herbs or sesame seeds, if desired.

Nutrition Information (per serving, recipe serves 4)
Calories: 143, Protein: 5g, Fat: 10g, Carbohydrates: 12g, Fiber: 5g, Sugar: 2g, Sodium: 88mg

Cheesy Baked Cauliflower

Ingredients:
- 1 head cauliflower, cut into florets
- 1/4 cup butter
- 1/4 cup all-purpose flour
- 2 cups milk
- 1 cup shredded cheddar cheese
- 1/4 cup grated Parmesan cheese
- 1/4 teaspoon garlic powder
- Salt and pepper, to taste
- Optional: chopped fresh parsley for garnish

Instructions:
1. Preheat the oven to 375°F (190°C).
2. Bring a large pot of salted water to a boil. Add the cauliflower florets and cook until tender, about 5-7 minutes. Drain well and set aside.
3. In a separate saucepan, melt the butter over medium heat. Whisk in the flour to make a roux. Cook, whisking constantly, for 1-2 minutes.
4. Slowly whisk in the milk, stirring constantly to prevent lumps from forming. Bring the mixture to a boil, then reduce the heat and simmer until the sauce has thickened, about 5-7 minutes.
5. Stir in the cheddar cheese, Parmesan cheese, garlic powder, salt, and pepper until the cheese is melted and the sauce is smooth.
6. Add the cooked cauliflower to the cheese sauce and stir to coat.

7. Transfer the mixture to a baking dish and bake in the preheated oven for 20-25 minutes, or until the top is golden brown and the cauliflower is heated through.
8. Garnish with chopped fresh parsley, if desired.

Nutrition Information (per serving, recipe serves 6)

Calories: 237, Protein: 11g, Fat: 15g, Carbohydrates: 16g, Fiber: 3g, Sugar: 7g, Sodium: 370mg

Quick and Easy Vegetarian Recipes for Busy Weeknights

One-Pot Vegetarian Chili

Ingredients:
- 1 tablespoon olive oil
- 1 large onion, chopped
- 4 cloves garlic, minced
- 1 red bell pepper, chopped
- 1 green bell pepper, chopped
- 2 tablespoons chili powder
- 1 teaspoon ground cumin
- 1/2 teaspoon smoked paprika
- 1/4 teaspoon cayenne pepper (optional)
- 1 (14-ounce) can diced tomatoes, undrained
- 1 (15-ounce) can black beans, drained and rinsed
- 1 (15-ounce) can kidney beans, drained and rinsed
- 1 (15-ounce) can corn, drained
- 1 cup vegetable broth
- Salt and black pepper, to taste
- Optional toppings: shredded cheddar cheese, sour cream, chopped green onions, cilantro

Instructions:
1. In a large Dutch oven, heat the olive oil over average heat.
2. Add the chopped onion and cook for 3-4 minutes until it begins to soften.
3. Add the minced garlic and cook for an additional minute.
4. Add the chopped bell peppers and cook for 5-6 minutes until they start to soften.

5. Add the chili powder, ground cumin, smoked paprika, and cayenne pepper (if using) and stir to combine.
6. Add the diced tomatoes (with their juices), black beans, kidney beans, corn, and vegetable broth to the pot.
7. Stir to combine everything and bring the mixture to a simmer.
8. Reduce the heat to low and let the chili simmer for 20-25 minutes, stirring occasionally.
9. Taste and add salt and black pepper as needed.
10. Serve the chili hot, topped with shredded cheddar cheese, sour cream, chopped green onions, and cilantro (if desired).

Nutritional value per serving (per serving, recipe serves 6))

Calories: 279, Fat: 5g, Carbohydrates: 50g, Fiber: 14g, Protein: 14g, Sodium: 767mg

15-Minute Vegetarian Pad Thai

Ingredients:
- 4 ounces flat rice noodles
- 2 tablespoons vegetable oil
- 2 cloves garlic, minced
- 1/2 cup diced tofu
- 2 eggs, lightly beaten
- 2 tablespoons brown sugar
- 2 tablespoons soy sauce
- 1 tablespoon rice vinegar
- 1 tablespoon lime juice
- 1/4 teaspoon red pepper flakes (optional)
- 1 cup bean sprouts
- 2 green onions, chopped
- 1/4 cup chopped peanuts
- Lime wedges, for serving

Instructions:
1. Cook the rice noodles. Drain and set aside.
2. In a large skillet or wok, heat the vegetable oil over medium-high heat.
3. Add the minced garlic and diced tofu to the skillet and cook for 1-2 minutes until the garlic is fragrant and the tofu is lightly browned.
4. Push the tofu and garlic to one side of the skillet and pour the beaten eggs into the other side. Scramble the eggs until they are fully cooked, then mix them with the tofu and garlic.

5. Add the cooked rice noodles to the skillet and stir to combine with the tofu and eggs.
6. In a small bowl, whisk together the soy sauce, brown sugar, rice vinegar, lime juice, and red pepper flakes (if using).
7. Pour the sauce over the noodle mixture and stir to combine everything.
8. Add the bean sprouts and green onions to the skillet and stir to combine.
9. Cook for an additional 1-2 minutes until the bean sprouts are slightly wilted and the green onions are softened.
10. Serve the Pad Thai hot, topped with chopped peanuts and lime wedges on the side.

Nutritional value per serving:

Calories: 568, Fat: 32g, Carbohydrates: 57g, Fiber: 5g, Protein: 18g, Sodium: 1,334mg

Sheet Pan Vegetable Fajitas

Ingredients:
- 1 red bell pepper, sliced
- 1 green bell pepper, sliced
- 1 yellow onion, sliced
- 1 zucchini, sliced
- 1 yellow squash, sliced
- 2 tablespoons olive oil
- 2 teaspoons chili powder
- 1 teaspoon ground cumin
- 1/2 teaspoon garlic powder
- 1/2 teaspoon smoked paprika
- Salt and black pepper, to taste
- 8 small flour tortillas
- Optional toppings: shredded cheddar cheese, salsa, guacamole, sour cream

Instructions:
1. Preheat the oven to 400°F (200°C).
2. In a large bowl, combine the sliced red bell pepper, green bell pepper, yellow onion, zucchini, and yellow squash.
3. Drizzle the olive oil over the vegetables and toss to coat.
4. In a bowl, mix together the chili powder, ground cumin, garlic powder, smoked paprika, salt, and black pepper.
5. Sprinkle the spice mixture over the vegetables and toss to coat evenly.
6. Spread the vegetables out on a large sheet pan and roast in the preheated oven for 2025 minutes, stirring once halfway

through, until the vegetables are tender and lightly browned.
7. While the vegetables are roasting, warm the flour tortillas in the microwave or on a griddle.
8. Serve the roasted vegetables hot, wrapped in the warm flour tortillas, and topped with shredded cheddar cheese, salsa, guacamole, and/or sour cream as desired.

Nutritional value per serving:

Calories: 263, Fat: 10, Carbohydrates: 38g, Fiber: 6g, Protein: 7g, Sodium: 426mg

Chickpea Salad Sandwiches

Ingredients:

- 2 cans (15 ounces each) chickpeas, drained and rinsed
- 1/2 cup diced red onion
- 1/2 cup diced celery
- 1/2 cup diced red bell pepper
- 1/4 cup chopped fresh parsley
- 1/4 cup mayonnaise
- 1 tablespoon Dijon mustard
- 1 tablespoon lemon juice
- 1/2 teaspoon garlic powder
- Salt and black pepper, to taste
- 8 slices whole wheat bread
- Lettuce leaves and sliced tomato, for serving (optional)

Instructions:

1. In a large bowl, mash the chickpeas with a potato masher until they are mostly broken
1. down but still have some texture.
2. Add the diced red onion, celery, red bell pepper, and chopped parsley to the bowl and stir to combine.
3. In a small bowl, whisk together the mayonnaise, Dijon mustard, lemon juice, garlic powder, salt, and black pepper.
4. Pour the dressing over the chickpea mixture and stir to coat everything evenly.
5. Toast the slices of whole wheat bread.

6. Bring together the sandwiches by spreading the chickpea salad mixture on four slices of bread. Top each with lettuce leaves and sliced tomato (if using), then place another slice of bread on top.
7. Serve the sandwiches immediately, or wrap them tightly in plastic wrap and store in the refrigerator for up to 2 days.

Nutritional value per serving:

Calories: 364, Fat: 14g, Carbohydrates: 47g, Fiber: 13g, Protein: 16g, Sodium: 772mg

Creamy Avocado and White Bean Wrap

Ingredients:
- 1 can (15 ounces) white beans, drained and rinsed
- 1 ripe avocado, pitted and peeled
- 1/4 cup plain Greek yogurt
- 2 tablespoons chopped fresh cilantro
- 1 tablespoon lime juice
- 1/2 teaspoon garlic powder
- Salt and black pepper, to taste
- 4 large whole wheat wraps
- 2 cups baby spinach leaves
- 1 cup cherry tomatoes, halved

Instructions:
1. In a medium bowl, mash the white beans with a fork or potato masher until they are mostly broken down but still have some texture.
2. In a separate bowl, mash the avocado until smooth.
3. Add the mashed avocado, Greek yogurt, chopped cilantro, lime juice, garlic powder, salt, and black pepper to the bowl with the white beans and stir to combine.
4. Warm the whole wheat wraps in the microwave or on a griddle.
5. To pull together the wraps, spread the avocado and white bean mixture evenly over each wrap.
6. Top each wrap with a handful of baby spinach leaves and some cherry tomato halves.
7. Roll up the wraps tightly and slice in half.

8. Serve the wraps immediately, or wrap them tightly in plastic wrap and store in the refrigerator for up to 2 days.

Nutritional value per serving:

Calories: 307, Fat: 12g, Carbohydrates: 39g, Fiber: 14g, Protein: 14g, Sodium: 370mg

Budget-Friendly Vegetarian Recipes

Lentil and Sweet Potato Shepherd's Pie

Ingredients:

- 2 large sweet potatoes, peeled and diced
- 1/4 cup unsweetened almond milk
- 2 tbsp olive oil
- 1 onion, chopped
- 3 garlic cloves, minced
- 2 carrots, chopped
- 2 celery stalks, chopped
- 1 cup brown or green lentils, rinsed
- 2 cups vegetable broth
- 1 tbsp tomato paste
- 1 tsp dried thyme
- Salt and pepper, to taste
- 1/4 cup nutritional yeast (optional)

Instructions:

1. Preheat oven to 375°F (190°C).
2. Place diced sweet potatoes in a pot and cover with water. Bring to a boil and cook until tender, about 10 minutes.
3. Drain sweet potatoes and add almond milk. Mash until smooth and set aside.
4. In a Dutch oven, heat olive oil over medium heat.
5. Add onion and garlic and cook until onion is translucent, about 5 minutes.
6. Add carrots and celery and cook for another 5 minutes.

7. Add lentils, vegetable broth, tomato paste, thyme, salt, and pepper to the skillet. Bring to a boil, then reduce heat and simmer for 20-25 minutes or until lentils are tender and most of the liquid is absorbed.
8. Transfer lentil mixture to a baking dish and spread mashed sweet potatoes over the top.
9. Bake for 20-25 minutes or until the top is golden brown.
10. Optional: sprinkle nutritional yeast over the top of the sweet potatoes for added flavor and nutrition.

Nutritional information (per serving)

Calories: 330, Fat: 8g, Carbohydrates: 53g, Fiber: 16g, Protein: 13g, Sodium: 360mg

Roasted Vegetable and Chickpea Salad

Ingredients:
- 1 red bell pepper, chopped
- 1 yellow bell pepper, chopped
- 1 small red onion, chopped
- 2 medium zucchini, chopped
- 1 can (15 oz) chickpeas, rinsed and drained
- 2 tbsp olive oil
- 1 tsp dried oregano
- Salt and pepper, to taste
- 4 cups mixed greens
- 1/4 cup crumbled feta cheese (optional)

For the dressing:
- 3 tbsp olive oil
- 1 tbsp lemon juice
- 1 tsp honey
- 1 tsp Dijon mustard
- Salt and pepper, to taste

Instructions:
1. Preheat oven to 425°F (220°C).
2. In a large bowl, combine chopped red and yellow bell peppers, red onion, zucchini, chickpeas, olive oil, oregano, salt, and pepper. Toss to coat.
3. Spread vegetables and chickpeas in a single layer on a baking sheet. Roast in the oven for 20-25 minutes or until vegetables are tender and slightly charred.

4. While the vegetables are roasting, make the dressing by whisking together olive oil, lemon juice, honey, Dijon mustard, salt, and pepper in a small bowl.
5. In a large bowl, toss mixed greens with the dressing.
6. Once the vegetables are roasted, let them cool for a few minutes before adding them to the mixed greens. Toss to combine.
7. Optional: sprinkle crumbled feta cheese over the top of the salad.

Nutritional information (per serving):

Calories: 360, Fat: 22g, Carbohydrates: 32g, Fiber: 9g, Protein: 9g, Sodium: 320mg

Stuffed Bell Peppers

Ingredients:

- 4 bell peppers (any color), halved and seeded
- 1 cup quinoa, rinsed
- 2 cups vegetable broth
- 1 tbsp olive oil
- 1 onion, chopped
- 3 garlic cloves, minced
- 1 zucchini, chopped
- 1 cup canned diced tomatoes
- 1 tsp dried basil
- 1 tsp dried oregano
- Salt and pepper, to taste
- 1/4 cup grated Parmesan cheese (optional)

Instructions:

1. Preheat oven to 375°F (190°C).
2. In a medium pot, bring quinoa and vegetable broth to a boil. Reduce heat, cover, and simmer for 15-20 minutes or until quinoa is tender and most of the liquid is absorbed.
3. In a large skillet, heat olive oil over medium heat.
4. Add onion and garlic and cook about 5 minutes.
5. Add chopped zucchini, diced tomatoes, dried basil, dried oregano, salt, and pepper to the skillet. Cook for another 5-7 minutes or until zucchini is tender.
6. Add cooked quinoa to the skillet and stir to combine.
7. Fill each bell pepper half with the quinoa and vegetable mixture.

8. Place stuffed bell peppers in a baking dish and cover with foil.
9. Bake for 30-35 minutes or until bell peppers are tender.

Nutritional information (per serving)

Calories: 290, Fat: 7g, Carbohydrates: 46g, Fiber: 10g, Protein: 11g, Sodium: 520mg

Three-Bean Chili

Ingredients:
- 1 tbsp olive oil
- 1 onion, chopped
- 3 garlic cloves, minced
- 1 red bell pepper, chopped
- 1 green bell pepper, chopped
- 1 jalapeño pepper, seeded and minced
- 2 tbsp chili powder
- 1 tbsp ground cumin
- 1 tsp smoked paprika
- 1 can (28 oz) diced tomatoes, undrained
- 1 can (15 oz) kidney beans, rinsed and drained
- 1 can (15 oz) black beans, rinsed and drained
- 1 can (15 oz) pinto beans, rinsed and drained
- 1 cup vegetable broth
- Salt and pepper, to taste
- Optional toppings: shredded cheddar cheese, sour cream, chopped cilantro

Instructions:
1. In a large pot, heat olive oil over medium heat.
2. Add onion and garlic and cook until onion is translucent, about 5 minutes.
3. Add red and green bell peppers and jalapeño pepper. Cook for another 5 minutes or until peppers are tender.

4. Add cumin, chili powder, smoked paprika, diced tomatoes (with their juice), kidney beans, black beans, pinto beans, and vegetable broth to the pot. Stir to combine.
5. Bring chili to a simmer and cook for 20-25 minutes, stirring occasionally.
6. Season with salt and pepper to taste.
7. Optional: top with shredded cheddar cheese, a dollop of sour cream, and/or chopped cilantro.

Nutritional information (per serving)

Calories: 320, Fat: 4g, Carbohydrates: 56g, Fiber: 20g, Protein: 18g, Sodium: 780mg

Spinach and Ricotta Stuffed Shells

Ingredients:
- 20 jumbo pasta shells
- 2 cups ricotta cheese
- 1 cup chopped fresh spinach
- 1 egg
- 1/4 cup grated Parmesan cheese
- 1 tbsp chopped fresh basil
- 1 garlic clove, minced
- Salt and pepper, to taste
- 1 jar (24 oz) tomato sauce
- 1 cup shredded mozzarella cheese

Instructions:
1. Preheat oven to 375°F (190°C).
2. Cook jumbo pasta shells as the package direct. Drain and rinse under cold water.
3. In a medium bowl, combine ricotta cheese, chopped spinach, egg, Parmesan cheese, basil, garlic, salt, and pepper.
4. Spread ½ cup tomato sauce on the bottom of a baking dish.
5. Stuff each pasta shell with the ricotta mixture and place in the baking dish.
6. Pour remaining tomato sauce over the top of the stuffed shells.
7. Using foil to cover the baking dish and bake for 25-30 minutes.

8. Remove foil and sprinkle shredded mozzarella cheese over the top of the stuffed shells.
9. Bake for an additional 10-15 minutes or until cheese is melted and bubbly.

Nutritional information (per serving)

Calories: 330, Fat: 14g, Carbohydrates: 32g, Fiber: 3g, Protein: 20g, Sodium: 780mg

Meal Prep Vegetarian Recipes for Weight Loss

Mason Jar Salads

Ingredients:
- 1/4 cup uncooked quinoa
- 1/2 cup canned chickpeas, rinsed and drained
- 1/2 cup cherry tomatoes, halved
- 1/2 cup cucumber, chopped
- 1/4 cup red onion, chopped
- 1/4 cup crumbled feta cheese
- 2 cups mixed greens
- 2 tablespoons olive oil
- 2 tablespoons balsamic vinegar
- Salt and pepper to taste

Instructions:
1. Cook the quinoa according to package instructions and let it cool.
2. In a Mason jar, layer the ingredients in the following order: quinoa, chickpeas, cherry tomatoes, cucumber, red onion, feta cheese, and mixed greens.
3. Drizzle olive oil and balsamic vinegar on top, and season with salt and pepper to taste.
4. Seal the Mason jar and store in the fridge until ready to eat.
5. When ready to eat, shake the Mason jar to mix all the ingredients together.

Nutritional information per serving (1 Mason jar salad)
Calories: 430, Protein: 16g, Fat: 24g, Carbohydrates: 39g, Fiber: 8g, Sugar: 7g, Sodium: 440mg

Quinoa and Black Bean Bowls

Ingredients:
- 1 cup uncooked quinoa
- 2 cups vegetable broth
- 1 can (15 oz) black beans, rinsed and drained
- 1 red bell pepper, chopped
- 1 yellow bell pepper, chopped
- 1 avocado, diced
- 1/4 cup red onion, chopped
- 1/4 cup cilantro, chopped
- Juice of 1 lime
- 2 tablespoons olive oil
- Salt and pepper to taste

Instructions:
1. Rinse the quinoa and combine it with the vegetable broth in a pot. Bring to a boil, reduce heat to low, cover, and simmer for 15-20 minutes until the quinoa is cooked and the liquid is absorbed. Let it cool.
2. In a bowl, mix together the black beans, cooked quinoa, bell peppers, avocado, red onion, and cilantro.
3. In a separate bowl, whisk together the lime juice, olive oil, salt, and pepper to make the dressing.
4. Pour the dressing over the quinoa and black bean mixture and toss to combine.
5. Serve immediately, or store in the fridge for up to 3 days.

Nutritional information per serving (1 bowl)
Calories: 470, Protein: 15g, Fat: 21g, Carbohydrates: 61g, Fiber: 17g, Sugar: 6g, Sodium: 690mg

Tofu and Broccoli Stir Fry

Ingredients:
- 1 block (14 oz) firm tofu, drained and pressed
- 3 cups broccoli florets
- 1 ed bell pepper, chopped
- 1/4 cup soy sauce
- 2 tablespoons cornstarch1 tablespoon honey
- 2 tablespoons sesame oil
- 2 cloves garlic, minced
- 1/4 teaspoon red pepper flakes (optional)
- Salt and pepper to taste

Instructions:
1. Cut the pressed tofu into 1-inch cubes and set aside.
2. In a small bowl, mix together the cornstarch, soy sauce, honey, and 1/4 cup of water to make the sauce.
3. Heat the sesame oil in a large skillet or wok over medium-high heat.
4. Add the garlic and red pepper flakes (if using) and sauté for 30 seconds until fragrant.
5. Add the tofu to the skillet and cook for 5-7 minutes, flipping occasionally, until golden brown.
6. Add the broccoli and bell pepper to the skillet and sauté for another 5 minutes until the vegetables are tender but still crisp.
7. Pour the sauce into the skillet and stir everything together until the sauce has thickened and coated the tofu and vegetables.

8. Season with salt and pepper to taste and serve immediately.

Nutritional information per serving (1/4 of the recipe)

Calories: 300, Protein: 19g, Fat: 16g, Carbohydrates: 23g, Fiber: 5g, Sugar: 9g, Sodium: 1200mg

Stuffed Sweet Potatoes

Ingredients:

- 4 medium sweet potatoes
- 1 can (15 oz) black beans, rinsed and drained
- 1 cup corn kernels
- 1/4 cup red onion, chopped
- 1/4 cup cilantro, chopped
- Juice of 1 lime
- 1 tablespoon olive oil
- 1 teaspoon cumin
- Salt and pepper to taste
- Optional toppings: avocado, salsa, sour cream, shredded cheese

Instructions:

1. Preheat the oven to 400°F (200°C).
2. Scrub the sweet potatoes and pierce them a few times with a fork. Place them on a baking sheet and bake for 45-60 minutes until they are soft and tender.
3. In a bowl, mix together the corn, black beans, red onion, cilantro, lime juice, olive oil, cumin, salt, and pepper.
4. Once the sweet potatoes are cooked, slice them in half lengthwise and scoop out a bit of the flesh from the center to make room for the filling.
5. Spoon the black bean and corn mixture into the sweet potato halves, filling them evenly.
6. Return the stuffed sweet potatoes to the oven and bake for another 10-15 minutes until the filling is heated through.

7. Serve immediately with optional toppings as desired.

Nutritional information per serving (1 stuffed sweet potato)

Calories: 330, Protein: 10g, Fat: 5g, Carbohydrates: 64g, Fiber: 14g, Sugar: 14g, Sodium: 250mg

Greek Yogurt Parfaits

Ingredients:

2 cups plain Greek yogurt

2 cups mixed berries (such as strawberries, blueberries, and raspberries)

1/4 cup honey

1/4 cup granola

2 tablespoons chopped nuts (such as almonds or walnuts)

Optional toppings: additional honey, cinnamon, shredded coconut

Instructions:
1. Wash the berries and slice any large ones into bite-sized pieces.
2. In a small bowl, mix together the honey and Greek yogurt until smooth.
3. In four serving glasses or jars, layer the Greek yogurt mixture, berries, and granola.
4. Repeat the layering until the glasses is filled up, ending with a layer of berries and granola on top.
5. Sprinkle the chopped nuts on top of each parfait.
6. Serve immediately, or store in the fridge for up to 2 days.

Nutritional information per serving (1 parfait)

Calories: 280, Protein: 18g, Fat: 5g, Carbohydrates: 47g, Fiber: 5g, Sugar: 39g, Sodium: 80mg

www.ingramcontent.com/pod-product-compliance
Lightning Source LLC
Chambersburg PA
CBHW071501080526
44587CB00014B/2175